CLASSIC SERIES

Greatest Ghost Stories

Published by:

V&S PUBLISHERS

F-2/16, Ansari road, Daryaganj, New Delhi-110002
☎ 23240026, 23240027 • *Fax:* 011-23240028
Email: info@vspublishers.com • *Website:* www.vspublishers.com

Regional Office : Hyderabad
5-1-707/1, Brij Bhawan (Beside Central Bank of India Lane)
Bank Street, Koti, Hyderabad - 500 095
☎ 040-24737290
E-mail: vspublishershyd@gmail.com

Branch Office : Mumbai
Godown # 34 at The Model Co-Operative Housing, Society Ltd.,
"Sahakar Niwas", Ground Floor, Next to Sobo Central, Mumbai - 400 034
E-mail: vspublishersmum@gmail.com

Follow us on:

For any assistance sms **VSPUB** to **56161**

All books available at **www.vspublishers.com**

© Copyright: V&S PUBLISHERS
ISBN 978-93-505710-2-6
Edition 2014

The Copyright of this book, as well as all matter contained herein (including illustrations) rests with the Publishers. No person shall copy the name of the book, its title design, matter and illustrations in any form and in any language, totally or partially or in any distorted form. Anybody doing so shall face legal action and will be responsible for damages.

Printed at : Param Offseters, Okhla, New Delhi-110020

Publisher's Note

It has been our constant endeavour at the **V&S Publishers** to publish all kinds of books ranging from Fiction, Non-fiction, Storybooks, Children Encyclopaedias, to Self-Help, Science Books, Dictionaries, Grammar Books, Self-Development, Management Books, etc.

However, this is for the first time that we are venturing into the vast, rich and fathomless ocean of English Literature and have come up with a set *of ten storybooks called the Greatest Classic Series* authored by some of the greatest and eminent writers of the world. There is a lot to learn from their writing style, selection of plot, development and building of theme and suspense of the story, emphasis and presentation of characters, dialogues, working towards the climax of the story, presenting the climax, and then finally concluding the story.

Each these books are of about 200 pages containing around ten popular stories or more of renowned authors like Oscar Wilde, Ernest William Hornung, Guy de Maupassant, O. Henry, Saki, Washington Irving, Thomas Hardy, Charles Dickens, Jules Verne, Jack London, Mark Twain, Edgar Allen Poe, H.G.Wells, Ambrose Bierce, Amelia Edwards, Edith Wharton, Wilkie Collins and many more. The series is called The Greatest Classic Series as all the names of the books begin with the word, 'Greatest' like the Greatest Adventurous Stories, Greatest Detective Stories, Greatest Love Stories, Greatest Ghost Stories, and so on. Besides this, three of the ten books are exclusively on the Adventures of Sherlock Holmes, one of the best detectives the world has ever known written by none other than Sir Arthur Conan Doyle.

Besides the above mentioned characteristics, the books contain an introductory page before each story introducing the author, his brief life history, notable works and literary achievements. Each story has a set of word meanings on each page followed by an exercise meant exclusively aiming the school students to help them grasp the essence of the story easily and quickly.

These books are not only a boon for the school-going students, particularly studying in senior classes from the seventh standard till the twelfth, but are also a treasure trove for all those young and aspiring writers, voracious readers and lovers of English language and literature.

Each of these ten books focus on a theme, such as adventure, love, terror, humour, or supernatural happenings, and are so captivating and real to life that readers may find it difficult to choose from them and so it's better to pick the entire series.

Wishing you all a happy and enjoyable reading...

Contents

Publisher's Note 3

Afterward 7
Sir Edmund Orme 38
The Phantom Coach 68
Mrs. Zant and the Ghost 84
The Secret of Macarger's Gulch 121
The Moonlit Road 130
The Haunted Valley 141
The Death of Halpin Frayser 154
The Striding Place 171

Afterward
~ Edith Wharton

I

"Oh, there one, of course, but you'll never know it."

The assertion, laughingly flung out six months earlier in a bright June garden, came back to Mary Boyne with a sharp perception of its latent significance as she stood, in the December dusk, waiting for the lamps to be brought into the library.

The words had been spoken by their friend Alida Stair, as they sat at tea on her lawn at Pangbourne, in reference to the very house of which the library in question was the central, the pivotal "feature." Mary Boyne and her husband, in quest of a country place in one of the southern or southwestern counties, had, on their arrival in England, carried their problem straight to Alida Stair, who had successfully solved it in her own case; but it was not until they had rejected, almost capriciously, several practical and judicious suggestions that she threw it out: "Well, there's Lyng, in Dorsetshire. It belongs to Hugo's cousins, and you can get it for a song."

The reasons she gave for its being obtainable on these terms -- its remoteness from a station, its lack of electric light, hot-water pipes, and other vulgar necessities -- were exactly those pleading in its favor with two romantic Americans perversely in search of the economic drawbacks which were associated, in their tradition, with unusual architectural felicities.

"I should never believe I was living in an old house unless I was thoroughly uncomfortable," Ned Boyne, the more extravagant of the two, had jocosely insisted; "the least hint of 'convenience' would make me think it had been bought out of an exhibition, with the pieces numbered, and set up again." And they had proceeded to enumerate, with humorous precision, their various suspicions and exactions, refusing to believe that the house their cousin recommended was Tudor till they learned it had no heating system, or that the village church was literally in the grounds till she assured them of the deplorable uncertainty of the water supply.

Assertion- *Contention claim*
Perception - *Awareness*
Pivotal - *Important*
Felicitie - *Happiness, joy*
Extravagant- *Spendthrift*
Jocosely- *Jokingly*
Deplorable - *Lamentable*

Greatest Ghost Stories

"It's too uncomfortable to be true!" Edward Boyne had continued to exult as the avowal of each disadvantage was successively wrung from her; but he had cut short his rhapsody to ask, with a sudden relapse to distrust: "And the ghost? You've been concealing from us the fact that there is no ghost!"

Mary, at the moment, had laughed with him, yet almost with her laugh, being possessed of several sets of independent perceptions, had noted a sudden flatness of tone in Alida's answering hilarity.

"Oh, Dorsetshire's full of ghosts, you know."

"Yes, yes; but that won't do. I don't want to have to drive ten miles to see somebody else's ghost. I want one of my own on the premises. there a ghost at Lyng?"

His rejoinder had made Alida laugh again, and it was then that she had flung back tantalizingly: "Oh, there one, of course, but you'll never know it."

"Never know it?" Boyne pulled her up. "But what in the world constitutes a ghost except the fact of its being known for one?"

"I can't say. But that's the story."

"That there's a ghost, but that nobody knows it's a ghost?"

"Well -- not till afterward, at any rate."

"Till afterward?"

"Not till long, long afterward."

"But if it's once been identified as an unearthly visitant, why hasn't its signalement been handed down in the family? How has it managed to preserve its incognito?"

Alida could only shake her head. "Don't ask me. But it has."

"And then suddenly --" Mary spoke up as if from some cavernous depth of divination --"suddenly, long afterward, one says to one's self,' '"

She was oddly startled at the sepulchral sound with which her question fell on the banter of the other two, and she saw the shadow of the same surprise flit across Alida's clear pupils. "I suppose so. One just has to wait."

"Oh, hang waiting!" Ned broke in. "Life's too short for a ghost who can only be enjoyed in retrospect. Can't we do better than that, Mary?"

But it turned out that in the event they were not destined to, for within three months of their conversation with Mrs. Stair

Exult - *Delight, glory*
Rhapsody - *An epic poem*
Hilarity - *Cheerfulness*
Tantalizingly - *Tea singly*
Signalement - *A detailed description of a Person*
Cavernous - *Deep-set, hollow but deep*

Greatest Ghost

they were established at Lyng, and the life they had yearned for to the point of planning it out in all its daily details had actually begun for them. It was to sit, in the thick December dusk, by just such a wide hooded fireplace, under just such black oak rafters, with the sense that beyond the mullioned panes the downs were darkening to a deeper solitude: it was for the ultimate indulgence in such sensations that Mary Boyne had endured for nearly fourteen years the soul-deadening ugliness of the Middle West, and that Boyne had ground on doggedly at his engineering till, with a suddenness that still made her blink, the prodigious windfall of the Blue Star Mine had put them at a stroke in possession of life and the leisure to taste it. They had never for a moment meant their new state to be one of idleness; but they meant to give themselves only to harmonious activities. She had her vision of painting and gardening (against a background of gray walls), he dreamed of the production of his long-planned book on the "Economic Basis of Culture"; and with such absorbing work ahead no existence could be too sequestered; they could not get far enough from the world, or plunge deep enough into the past.

Dorsetshire had attracted them from the first by a semblance of remoteness out of all proportion to its geographical position. But to the Boynes it was one of the ever-recurring wonders of the whole incredibly compressed island -- a nest of counties, as they put it -- that for the production of its effects so little of a given quality went so far: that so few miles made a distance, and so short a distance a difference.

"It's that," Ned had once enthusiastically explained, "that gives such depth to their effects, such relief to their least contrasts. They've been able to lay the butter so thick on every exquisite mouthful."

The butter had certainly been laid on thick at Lyng: the old gray house, hidden under a shoulder of the downs, had almost all the finer marks of commerce with a protracted past. The mere fact that it was neither large nor exceptional made it, to the Boynes, abound the more richly in its special sense -- the sense of having been for centuries a deep, dim reservoir of life. The life had probably not been of the most vivid order: for long periods, no doubt, it had fallen as noiselessly into the past as the quiet drizzle of autumn fell, hour after hour, into the green fish-pond between the yews; but these back-waters of existence sometimes breed, in their sluggish depths, strange acuities of

Wide hooded- *Broad*
Sequestered - *To remove*
Protracted - *To extend*
Exceptional - *Extraordinary*
Acuities - *Keeness, Sharpness*

emotion, and Mary Boyne had felt from the first the occasional brush of an intenser memory.

The feeling had never been stronger than on the December afternoon when, waiting in the library for the belated lamps, she rose from her seat and stood among the shadows of the hearth. Her husband had gone off, after luncheon, for one of his long tramps on the downs. She had noticed of late that he preferred to be unaccompanied on these occasions; and, in the tried security of their personal relations, had been driven to conclude that his book was bothering him, and that he needed the afternoons to turn over in solitude the problems left from the morning's work. Certainly the book was not going as smoothly as she had imagined it would, and the lines of perplexity between his eyes had never been there in his engineering days. Then he had often looked fagged to the verge of illness, but the native demon of "worry" had never branded his brow. Yet the few pages he had so far read to her -- the introduction, and a synopsis of the opening chapter -- gave evidences of a firm possession of his subject, and a deepening confidence in his powers.

The fact threw her into deeper perplexity, since, now that he had done with "business" and its disturbing contingencies, the one other possible element of anxiety was eliminated. Unless it were his health, then? But physically he had gained since they had come to Dorsetshire, grown robuster, ruddier, and fresher-eyed. It was only within a week that she had felt in him the undefinable change that made her restless in his absence, and as tongue-tied in his presence as though it were who had a secret to keep from him!

The thought that there a secret somewhere between them struck her with a sudden smart rap of wonder, and she looked about her down the dim, long room.

"Can it be the house?" she mused.

The room itself might have been full of secrets. They seemed to be piling themselves up, as evening fell, like the layers and layers of velvet shadow dropping from the low ceiling, the dusky walls of books, the smoke-blurred sculpture of the hooded hearth.

"Why, of course -- the house is haunted!" she reflected.

The ghost -- Alida's imperceptible ghost -- after figuring largely in the banter of their first month or two at Lyng, had been gradually discarded as too ineffectual for imaginative

---

Intenser - *Occurring in a high degree*
Fagged - *Tired*
Contingencies - *Uncertainties*
Hearth - *The floor of a fire place*
Imperceptible - *Gradual*
Banter - *Playful, teasing remarks*

use. Mary had, indeed, as became the tenant of a haunted house, made the customary inquiries among her few rural neighbors, but, beyond a vague, "They du say so, Ma'am," the villagers had nothing to impart. The elusive spectre had apparently never had sufficient identity for a legend to crystallize about it, and after a time the Boynes had laughingly set the matter down to their profit and-loss account, agreeing that Lyng was one of the few houses good enough in itself to dispense with supernatural enhancements.

"And I suppose, poor, ineffectual demon, that's why it beats its beautiful wings in vain in the void," Mary had laughingly concluded.

"Or, rather," Ned answered, in the same strain, "why, amid so much that's ghostly, it can never affirm its separate existence as ghost." And thereupon their invisible housemate had finally dropped out of their references, which were numerous enough to make them promptly unaware of the loss.

Now, as she stood on the hearth, the subject of their earlier curiosity revived in her with a new sense of its meaning -- a sense gradually acquired through close daily contact with the scene of the lurking mystery. It was the house itself, of course, that possessed the ghost-seeing faculty, that communed visually but secretly with its own past; and if one could only get into close enough communion with the house, one might surprise its secret, and acquire the ghost-sight on one's own account. Perhaps, in his long solitary hours in this very room, where she never trespassed till the afternoon, her husband acquired it already, and was silently carrying the dread weight of whatever it had revealed to him. Mary was too well-versed in the code of the spectral world not to know that one could not talk about the ghosts one saw: to do so was almost as great a breach of goodbreeding as to name a lady in a club. But this explanation did not really satisfy her. "What, after all, except for the fun of the frisson," she reflected, "would he really care for any of their old ghosts?" And thence she was thrown back once more on the fundamental dilemma: the fact that one's greater or less susceptibility to spectral influences had no particular bearing on the case, since, when one see a ghost at Lyng, one did not know it.

"Not till long afterward," Alida Stair had said. Well, supposing Ned seen one when they first came, and had known only within the last week what had happened to him? More and

Elusive - *Difficult to express*
Spectre - *A ghost*
Apparently - *Readily visible*
Communed - *Talked intimately*
Trespassed - *Encorached on a person privacy*
Susceptibility - *Emotional sensibilities*

more under the spell of the hour, she threw back her searching thoughts to the early days of their tenancy, but at first only to recall a gay confusion of unpacking, settling, arranging of books, and calling to each other from remote corners of the house as treasure after treasure of their habitation revealed itself to them. It was in this particular connection that she presently recalled a certain soft afternoon of the previous October, when, passing from the first rapturous flurry of exploration to a detailed inspection of the old house, she had pressed (like a novel heroine) a panel that opened at her touch, on a narrow flight of stairs leading to an unsuspected flat ledge of the roof -- the roof which, from below, seemed to slope away on all sides too abruptly for any but practised feet to scale.

The view from this hidden coign was enchanting, and she had flown down to snatch Ned from his papers and give him the freedom of her discovery. She remembered still how, standing on the narrow ledge, he had passed his arm about her while their gaze flew to the long, tossed horizon-line of the downs, and then dropped contentedly back to trace the arabesque of yew hedges about the fish-pond, and the shadow of the cedar on the lawn.

"And now the other way," he had said, gently turning her about within his arm; and closely pressed to him, she had absorbed, like some long, satisfying draft, the picture of the gray-walled court, the squat lions on the gates, and the lime-avenue reaching up to the highroad under the downs.

It was just then, while they gazed and held each other, that she had felt his arm relax, and heard a sharp "Hullo!" that made her turn to glance at him.

Distinctly, yes, she now recalled she had seen, as she glanced, a shadow of anxiety, of perplexity, rather, fall across his face; and, following his eyes, had beheld the figure of a man -- a man in loose, greyish clothes, as it appeared to her -- who was sauntering down the lime-avenue to the court with the tentative gait of a stranger seeking his way. Her short-sighted eyes had given her but a blurred impression of slightness and grayness, with something foreign, or at least unlocal, in the cut of the figure or its garb; but her husband had apparently seen more -- seen enough to make him push past her with a sharp "Wait!" and dash down the twisting stairs without pausing to give her a hand for the descent.

Rapturous- *Expressing extreme pleasure*
Ledge - *Horizontal surface resembling a shelf*
Enchantige - *Charming*
Garb - *To clothe, dress, attire*

A slight tendency to dizziness obliged her, after a provisional clutch at the chimney against which they had been leaning, to follow him down more cautiously; and when she had reached the attic landing she paused again for a less definite reason, leaning over the oak banister to strain her eyes through the silence of the brown, sun-flecked depths below. She lingered there till, somewhere in those depths, she heard the closing of a door; then, mechanically impelled, she went down the shallow flights of steps till she reached the lower hall.

The front door stood open on the mild sunlight of the court, and hall and court were empty. The library door was open, too, and after listening in vain for any sound of voices within, she quickly crossed the threshold, and found her husband alone, vaguely fingering the papers on his desk.

He looked up, as if surprised at her precipitate entrance, but the shadow of anxiety had passed from his face, leaving it even, as she fancied, a little brighter and clearer than usual.

"What was it? Who was it?" she asked.

"Who?" he repeated, with the surprise still all on his side.

"The man we saw coming toward the house."

He seemed honestly to reflect. "The man? Why, I thought I saw Peters; I dashed after him to say a word about the stable-drains, but he had disappeared before I could get down."

"Disappeared? Why, he seemed to be walking so slowly when we saw him."

Boyne shrugged his shoulders. "So I thought; but he must have got up steam in the interval. What do you say to our trying a scramble up Meldon Steep before sunset?"

That was all. At the time the occurrence had been less than nothing, had, indeed, been immediately obliterated by the magic of their first vision from Meldon Steep, a height which they had dreamed of climbing ever since they had first seen its bare spine heaving itself above the low roof of Lyng. Doubtless it was the mere fact of the other incident's having occurred on the very day of their ascent to Meldon that had kept it stored away in the unconscious fold of association from which it now emerged; for in itself it had no mark of the ***portentous***. At the moment there could have been nothing more natural than that Ned should dash himself from the roof in the pursuit of ***dilatory*** tradesmen. It was the period

Dizziness - *Affected with a reeling sensation*
Cautiously - *Carefully*
Impelled - *Compelled*
Obliterated - *Destroyed completely*
Portentous - *Miraculous*
Dilatory - *Inclined to delay, defer decision*

when they were always on the watch for one or the other of the specialists employed about the place; always lying in wait for them, and dashing out at them with questions, reproaches, or reminders. And certainly in the distance the gray figure had looked like Peters.

Yet now, as she reviewed the rapid scene, she felt her husband's explanation of it to have been invalidated by the look of anxiety on his face. Why had the familiar appearance of Peters made him anxious? Why, above all, if it was of such prime necessity to confer with that authority on the subject of the stable-drains, had the failure to find him produced such a look of relief? Mary could not say that any one of these considerations had occurred to her at the time, yet, from the promptness with which they now marshalled themselves at her summons, she had a sudden sense that they must all along have been there, waiting their hour.

II

Weary with her thoughts, she moved toward the window. The library was now completely dark, and she was surprised to see how much faint light the outer world still held.

As she peered out into it across the court, a figure shaped itself in the tapering perspective of bare lines: it looked a mere blot of deeper gray in the greyness, and for an instant, as it moved toward her, her heart thumped to the thought, "It's the ghost!"

She had time, in that long instant, to feel suddenly that the man of whom, two months earlier, she had a brief distant vision from the roof was now, at his predestined hour, about to reveal himself as having been Peters; and her spirit sank under the impending fear of the disclosure. But almost with the next tick of the clock the ambiguous figure, gaining substance and character, showed itself even to her weak sight as her husband's; and she turned away to meet him, as he entered, with the confession of her folly.

"It's really too absurd," she laughed out from the threshold, "but I never remember!"

"Remember what?" Boyne questioned as they drew together.

"That when one sees the Lyng ghost one never knows it."

Reproaches - *To find, fault with person, blame*
Marshalled - *To arrange in proper order*
Predestined - *Determine before hand*
Impending - *Immenent*
Ambiguous - *Doubtful, obscure*
Absurd - *Silly, ridiculous*

Her hand was on his sleeve, and he kept it there, but with no response in his *gesture* or in the lines of his fagged, preoccupied face.

"Did you think you'd seen it?" he asked, after an appreciable interval.

"Why, I actually took for it, my dear, in my mad determination to spot it!"

"Me -- just now?" His arm dropped away, and he turned from her with a faint *echo* of her laugh. "Really, dearest, you'd better give it up, if that's the best you can do."

"Yes, I give it up -- I give it up. Have?" she asked, turning round on him *abruptly*.

The parlor-maid had entered with letters and a lamp, and the light struck up into Boyne's face as he bent above the tray she presented.

"Have?" Mary *perversely* insisted, when the servant had disappeared on her errand of illumination. "Have I what?" he rejoined absently, the light bringing out the sharp stamp of worry between his brows as he turned over the letters.

"Given up trying to see the ghost." Her heart beat a little at the experiment she was making.

Her husband, laying his letters aside, moved away into the shadow of the hearth.

"I never tried," he said, tearing open the wrapper of a newspaper.

"Well, of course," Mary persisted, "the exasperating thing is that there's no use trying, since one can't be sure till so long afterward."

He was unfolding the paper as if he had hardly heard her; but after a pause, during which the sheets rustled spasmodically between his hands, he lifted his head to say abruptly, "Have you any idea?"

Mary had sunk into a low chair beside the fireplace. From her seat she looked up, startled, at her husband's profile, which was darkly projected against the circle of lamplight.

"No; none. Have YOU?" she retorted, repeating her former phrase with an added keenness of intention. Boyne crumpled the paper into a bunch, and then inconsequently turned back with it toward the lamp.

Gesture - *To express with a motion of hands/body*
Abruptly - *Quickly*
Perversely - *Way hardly*
Persisted - *Continued*
Retorted - *Replied*
Inconsequently - *Irrelevantly*

"Lord, no! I only meant," he explained, with a faint tinge of impatience, "is there any legend, any tradition, as to that?"

"Not that I know of," she answered; but the impulse to add, "What makes you ask?" was checked by the reappearance of the parlourmaid with tea and a second lamp.

With the dispersal of shadows, and the repetition of the daily domestic office, Mary Boyne felt herself less oppressed by that sense of something mutely imminent which had darkened her solitary afternoon. For a few moments she gave herself silently to the details of her task, and when she looked up from it she was struck to the point of bewilderment by the change in her husband's face. He had seated himself near the farther lamp, and was absorbed in the perusal of his letters; but was it something he had found in them, or merely the shifting of her own point of view, that had restored his features to their normal aspect? The longer she looked, the more definitely the change affirmed itself. The lines of painful tension had vanished, and such traces of fatigue as lingered were of the kind easily attributable to steady mental effort. He glanced up, as if drawn by her gaze, and met her eyes with a smile.

"I'm dying for my tea, you know; and here's a letter for you," he said.

She took the letter he held out in exchange for the cup she proffered him, and, returning to her seat, broke the seal with the languid gesture of the reader whose interests are all inclosed in the circle of one cherished presence.

Her next conscious motion was that of starting to her feet, the letter falling to them as she rose, while she held out to her husband a long newspaper clipping.

"Ned! What's this? What does it mean?"

He had risen at the same instant, almost as if hearing her cry before she uttered it; and for a perceptible space of time he and she studied each other, like adversaries watching for an advantage, across the space between her chair and his desk.

"What's what? You fairly made me jump!" Boyne said at length, moving toward her with a sudden, half-exasperated laugh. The shadow of apprehension was on his face again, not now a look of fixed foreboding, but a shifting vigilance of lips and eyes that gave her the sense of his feeling himself invisibly surrounded.

Dispersal - *Spread*
Perusal - *Survey, examine*
Affirmed - *Confirmed*
Adversaries - *Oppenents*
Apprehension - *Guess, anticipation*

Her hand shook so that she could hardly give him the clipping.

"This article -- from the 'Waukesha Sentinel' -- that a man named Elwell has brought suit against you -- that there was something wrong about the Blue Star Mine. I can't understand more than half."

They continued to face each other as she spoke, and to her astonishment, she saw that her words had the almost immediate effect of dissipating the strained watchfulness of his look.

"Oh, !" He glanced down the printed slip, and then folded it with the gesture of one who handles something harmless and familiar. "What's the matter with you this afternoon, Mary? I thought you'd got bad news."

She stood before him with her undefinable terror subsiding slowly under the reassuring touch of his composure.

"You knew about this, then -- it's all right?"

"Certainly I knew about it; and it's all right."

"But what it? I don't understand. What does this man accuse you of?"

"Oh, pretty nearly every crime in the calendar." Boyne had tossed the clipping down, and thrown himself comfortably into an arm-chair near the fire. "Do you want to hear the story? It's not particularly interesting -- just a squabble over interests in the Blue Star."

"But who is this Elwell? I don't know the name."

"Oh, he's a fellow I put into it -- gave him a hand up. I told you all about him at the time."

"I daresay. I must have forgotten." Vainly she strained back among her memories. "But if you helped him, why does he make this return?"

"Oh, probably some shyster lawyer got hold of him and talked him over. It's all rather technical and complicated. I thought that kind of thing bored you."

His wife felt a sting of compunction. Theoretically, she deprecated the American wife's detachment from her husband's professional interests, but in practice she had always found it difficult to fix her attention on Boyne's report of the transactions in which his varied interests involved him. Besides, she had felt from the first that, in a community where the amenities of living could be obtained only at the cost of efforts as arduous as her

Dissipating - *To scatter*
Composure - *Serenity*
Squabble - *Petty quarrel*
Transactions - *Business Arduous deals laborious*

husband's professional labors, such brief leisure as they could command should be used as an escape from immediate preoccupations, a flight to the life they always dreamed of living. Once or twice, now that this new life had actually drawn its magic circle about them, she had asked herself if she had done right; but hitherto such conjectures had been no more than the retrospective excursions of an active fancy. Now, for the first time, it startled her a little to find how little she knew of the material foundation on which her happiness was built.

She glanced again at her husband, and was reassured by the composure of his face; yet she felt the need of more definite grounds for her reassurance.

"But doesn't this suit worry you? Why have you never spoken to me about it?"

He answered both questions at once: "I didn't speak of it at first because it worry me -- annoyed me, rather. But it's all ancient history now. Your correspondent must have got hold of a back number of the 'Sentinel.'"

She felt a quick thrill of relief. "You mean it's over? He's lost his case?"

There was a just perceptible delay in Boyne's reply. "The suit's been withdrawn -- that's all."

But she persisted, as if to exonerate herself from the inward charge of being too easily put off. "Withdrawn because he saw he had no chance?"

"Oh, he had no chance," Boyne answered.

She was still struggling with a dimly felt perplexity at the back of her thoughts.

"How long ago was it withdrawn?"

He paused, as if with a slight return of his former uncertainty. "I've just had the news now; but I've been expecting it."

"Just now -- in one of your letters?"

"Yes; in one of my letters."

She made no answer, and was aware only, after a short interval of waiting, that he had risen, and strolling across the room, had placed himself on the sofa at her side. She felt him, as he did so, pass an arm about her, she felt his hand seek hers and clasp it, and turning slowly, drawn by the warmth of his cheek, she met the smiling clearness of his eyes.

Retrospective - *Looking or directed backwards*
Conjectures *- Hypotheses, Suppositions*
Strolling - *Walking leisurely*

Greatest   Ghost   Stories

"It's all right -- it's all right?" she questioned, through the flood of her dissolving doubts; and "I give you my word it never was righter!" he laughed back at her, holding her close.

III

One of the strangest things she was afterward to recall out of all the next day's incredible strangeness was the sudden and complete recovery of her sense of security.

It was in the air when she woke in her low-ceilinged, dusky room; it accompanied her down-stairs to the breakfast-table, flashed out at her from the fire, and re-duplicated itself brightly from the flanks of the urn and the sturdy flutings of the Georgian teapot. It was as if, in some roundabout way, all her diffused apprehensions of the previous day, with their moment of sharp concentration about the newspaper article, -- as if this dim questioning of the future, and startled return upon the past,-had between them liquidated the arrears of some haunting moral obligation. If she had indeed been careless of her husband's affairs, it was, her new state seemed to prove, because her faith in him instinctively justified such carelessness; and his right to her faith had overwhelmingly affirmed itself in the very face of menace and suspicion. She had never seen him more untroubled, more naturally and unconsciously in possession of himself, than after the cross-examination to which she had subjected him: it was almost as if he had been aware of her lurking doubts, and had wanted the air cleared as much as she did.

It was as clear, thank Heaven! as the bright outer light that surprised her almost with a touch of summer when she issued from the house for her daily round of the gardens. She had left Boyne at his desk, indulging herself, as she passed the library door, by a last peep at his quiet face, where he bent, pipe in his mouth, above his papers, and now she had her own morning's task to perform. The task involved on such charmed winter days almost as much delighted loitering about the different quarters of her demesne as if spring were already at work on shrubs and borders. There were such inexhaustible possibilities still before her, such opportunities to bring out the latent graces of the old place, without a single irreverent touch of alteration, that the winter months were all too short to plan what spring and autumn executed. And her recovered sense of safety gave, on this

Flanks - *The sides of anything*
Apprehensions - *Suspicions*
Overwhelmingly - *Overpoweringly*
Loitering - *To roam about aimlessly*
Irreverent - *Irreligious*

particular morning, a peculiar zest to her progress through the sweet, still place. She went first to the kitchen-garden, where the espaliered pear-trees drew complicated patterns on the walls, and pigeons were fluttering and preening about the silvery-slated roof of their cot. There was something wrong about the piping of the hothouse, and she was expecting an authority from Dorchester, who was to drive out between trains and make a diagnosis of the boiler. But when she dipped into the damp heat of the greenhouses, among the spiced scents and waxy pinks and reds of old-fashioned exotics, -- even the flora of Lyng was in the note!-she learned that the great man had not arrived, and the day being too rare to waste in an artificial atmosphere, she came out again and paced slowly along the springy turf of the bowling-green to the gardens behind the house. At their farther end rose a grass terrace, commanding, over the fish-pond and the yew hedges, a view of the long house-front, with its twisted chimney-stacks and the blue shadows of its roof angles, all drenched in the pale gold moisture of the air.

Seen thus, across the level tracery of the yews, under the suffused, mild light, it sent her, from its open windows and hospitably smoking chimneys, the look of some warm human presence, of a mind slowly ripened on a sunny wall of experience. She had never before had so deep a sense of her intimacy with it, such a conviction that its secrets were all beneficent, kept, as they said to children, "for one's good," so complete a trust in its power to gather up her life and Ned's into the harmonious pattern of the long, long story it sat there weaving in the sun.

She heard steps behind her, and turned, expecting to see the gardener, accompanied by the engineer from Dorchester. But only one figure was in sight, that of a youngish, slightly built man, who, for reasons she could not on the spot have specified, did not remotely resemble her preconceived notion of an authority on hot-house boilers. The new-comer, on seeing her, lifted his hat, and paused with the air of a gentleman -- perhaps a traveler-desirous of having it immediately known that his intrusion is involuntary. The local fame of Lyng occasionally attracted the more intelligent sight-seer, and Mary half-expected to see the stranger dissemble a camera, or justify his presence by producing it. But he made no gesture of any sort, and after a moment she asked, in a tone responding to the courteous deprecation of his attitude: "Is there any one you wish to see?"

Exotics - *Having a strange beauty or quality*
Suffused - *Spread*
Harmonious - *Consistent, systematic*
Dissemble - *Hide, mask*
Hospitably - *Courteous fond of entertaining*

"I came to see Mr. Boyne," he replied. His intonation, rather than his accent, was faintly American, and Mary, at the familiar note, looked at him more closely. The brim of his soft felt hat cast a shade on his face, which, thus obscured, wore to her short-sighted gaze a look of seriousness, as of a person arriving "on business," and civilly but firmly aware of his rights.

Past experience had made Mary equally sensible to such claims; but she was jealous of her husband's morning hours, and doubtful of his having given any one the right to intrude on them. "Have you an appointment with Mr. Boyne?" she asked.

He hesitated, as if unprepared for the question.

"Not exactly an appointment," he replied.

"Then I'm afraid, this being his working-time, that he can't receive you now. Will you give me a message, or come back later?"

The visitor, again lifting his hat, briefly replied that he would come back later, and walked away, as if to regain the front of the house. As his figure receded down the walk between the yew hedges, Mary saw him pause and look up an instant at the peaceful house-front bathed in faint winter sunshine; and it struck her, with a tardy touch of compunction, that it would have been more humane to ask if he had come from a distance, and to offer, in that case, to inquire if her husband could receive him. But as the thought occurred to her he passed out of sight behind a pyramidal yew, and at the same moment her attention was distracted by the approach of the gardener, attended by the bearded pepper-and-salt figure of the boiler-maker from Dorchester.

The encounter with this authority led to such far-reaching issues that they resulted in his finding it expedient to ignore his train, and beguiled Mary into spending the remainder of the morning in absorbed confabulation among the greenhouses. She was startled to find, when the colloquy ended, that it was nearly luncheon-time, and she half expected, as she hurried back to the house, to see her husband coming out to meet her. But she found no one in the court but an under-gardener raking the gravel, and the hall, when she entered it, was so silent that she guessed Boyne to be still at work behind the closed door of the library.

Not wishing to disturb him, she turned into the drawing-room, and there, at her writing-table, lost herself in renewed calculations of the outlay to which the morning's conference had committed her. The knowledge that she could permit herself such follies had not yet lost its novelty; and somehow, in contrast

Intonation - *The pattern or melody of pitch of sound or voice*
Hedges - *A row of bushes*
Compunction - *A felling of uneasiness*
Distracted - *Attention diverted*
Encounter - *To meet with obscured vague not clear*
Confabulation - *To discuss, chat*

to the vague apprehensions of the previous days, it now seemed an element of her recovered security, of the sense that, as Ned had said, things in general had never been "righter."

She was still luxuriating in a lavish play of figures when the parlor-maid, from the threshold, roused her with a dubiously worded inquiry as to the expediency of serving luncheon. It was one of their jokes that Trimmle announced luncheon as if she were divulging a state secret, and Mary, intent upon her papers, merely murmured an absent-minded assent.

She felt Trimmle wavering expressively on the threshold as if in rebuke of such offhand acquiescence; then her retreating steps sounded down the passage, and Mary, pushing away her papers, crossed the hall, and went to the library door. It was still closed, and she wavered in her turn, disliking to disturb her husband, yet anxious that he should not exceed his normal measure of work. As she stood there, balancing her impulses, the esoteric Trimmle returned with the announcement of luncheon, and Mary, thus impelled, opened the door and went into the library.

Boyne was not at his desk, and she peered about her, expecting to discover him at the book-shelves, somewhere down the length of the room; but her call brought no response, and gradually it became clear to her that he was not in the library.

She turned back to the parlor-maid.

"Mr. Boyne must be up-stairs. Please tell him that luncheon is ready."

The parlor-maid appeared to hesitate between the obvious duty of obeying orders and an equally obvious conviction of the foolishness of the injunction laid upon her. The struggle resulted in her saying doubtfully, "If you please, Madam, Mr. Boyne's not up-stairs."

"Not in his room? Are you sure?"

"I'm sure, Madam."

Mary consulted the clock. "Where is he, then?"

"He's gone out," Trimmle announced, with the superior air of one who has respectfully waited for the question that a well-ordered mind would have first propounded.

Mary's previous conjecture had been right, then. Boyne must have gone to the gardens to meet her, and since she had missed him, it was clear that he had taken the shorter way by the south door, instead of going round to the court. She crossed the hall

---

Luxuriating -
Growing fully
Divulging -
Disclosing
Acquiescence - *To comply withy or assent to*
Wavered - *Be unsteady, shake or tremble*
Esoteric - *Confidential, secret*

to the glass portal opening directly on the yew garden, but the parlourmaid, after another moment of inner conflict, decided to bring out recklessly, "Please, Madam, Mr. Boyne didn't go that way."

Mary turned back. "Where he go? And when?"

"He went out of the front door, up the drive, Madam." It was a matter of principle with Trimmle never to answer more than one question at a time.

"Up the drive? At this hour?" Mary went to the door herself, and glanced across the court through the long tunnel of bare limes. But its perspective was as empty as when she had scanned it on entering the house.

"Did Mr. Boyne leave no message?" she asked.

Trimmle seemed to surrender herself to a last struggle with the forces of chaos.

"No, Madam. He just went out with the gentleman."

"The gentleman? What gentleman?" Mary wheeled about, as if to front this new factor.

"The gentleman who called, Madam," said Trimmle, resignedly.

"When did a gentleman call? Do explain yourself, Trimmle!"

Only the fact that Mary was very hungry, and that she wanted to consult her husband about the greenhouses, would have caused her to lay so unusual an injunction on her attendant; and even now she was detached enough to note in Trimmle's eye the dawning defiance of the respectful subordinate who has been pressed too hard.

"I couldn't exactly say the hour, Madam, because I didn't let the gentleman in," she replied, with the air of magnanimously ignoring the irregularity of her mistress's course.

"You didn't let him in?"

"No, Madam. When the bell rang I was dressing, and Agnes --"

"Go and ask Agnes, then," Mary interjected. Trimmle still wore her look of patient magnanimity. "Agnes would not know, Madam, for she had unfortunately burnt her hand in trying the *wick* of the new lamp from town --" Trimmle, as Mary was aware, had always been opposed to the new lamp --"and so Mrs. Dockett sent the kitchen-maid instead."

Conjecture -
Interjected inserted
Recklessly -
Negligently, rashly
Defiance - *Disregard*
Magnanimously -
Generously and noble

Mary looked again at the clock. "It's after two! Go and ask the kitchen-maid if Mr. Boyne left any word."

She went into luncheon without waiting, and Trimmle presently brought her there the kitchen-maid's statement that the gentleman had called about one o'clock, that Mr. Boyne had gone out with him without leaving any message. The kitchen-maid did not even know the caller's name, for he had written it on a slip of paper, which he had folded and handed to her, with the injunction to deliver it at once to Mr. Boyne.

Mary finished her luncheon, still wondering, and when it was over, and Trimmle had brought the coffee to the drawing-room, her wonder had deepened to a first faint tinge of disquietude. It was unlike Boyne to absent himself without explanation at so unwonted an hour, and the difficulty of identifying the visitor whose summons he had apparently obeyed made his disappearance the more unaccountable. Mary Boyne's experience as the wife of a busy engineer, subject to sudden calls and compelled to keep irregular hours, had trained her to the philosophic acceptance of surprises; but since Boyne's withdrawal from business he had adopted a Benedictine regularity of life. As if to make up for the dispersed and agitated years, with their "stand-up" lunches and dinners rattled down to the joltings of the dining-car, he cultivated the last refinements of punctuality and monotony, discouraging his wife's fancy for the unexpected; and declaring that to a delicate taste there were infinite gradations of pleasure in the fixed recurrences of habit.

Still, since no life can completely defend itself from the unforeseen, it was evident that all Boyne's precautions would sooner or later prove unavailable, and Mary concluded that he had cut short a tiresome visit by walking with his caller to the station, or at least accompanying him for part of the way.

This conclusion relieved her from farther preoccupation, and she went out herself to take up her conference with the gardener. Thence she walked to the village post-office, a mile or so away; and when she turned toward home, the early twilight was setting in.

She had taken a foot-path across the downs, and as Boyne, meanwhile, had probably returned from the station by the high-road, there was little likelihood of their meeting on the way. She felt sure, however, of his having reached the house before her;

Wick - *A bundle or loose twist of soft threads*
Injunction - *A command order*
Disquietude - *Anxiety*
Dispersed - *To spread*
Unforeseen - *To see beforehand*

so sure that, when she entered it herself, without even pausing to inquire of Trimmle, she made directly for the library. But the library was still empty, and with an unwanted precision of visual memory she immediately observed that the papers on her husband's desk lay precisely as they had lain when she had gone in to call him to luncheon.

Then of a sudden she was seized by a vague dread of the unknown. She had closed the door behind her on entering, and as she stood alone in the long, silent, shadowy room, her dread seemed to take shape and sound, to be there audibly breathing and lurking among the shadows. Her short-sighted eyes strained through them, halfdiscerning an actual presence, something aloof, that watched and knew; and in the recoil from that *in*tangible propinquity she threw herself suddenly on the bell-rope and gave it a desperate pull.

The long, quavering summons brought Trimmle in precipitately with a lamp, and Mary breathed again at this sobering reappearance of the usual.

"You may bring tea if Mr. Boyne is in," she said, to justify her ring.

"Very well, Madam. But Mr. Boyne is not in," said Trimmle, putting down the lamp.

"Not in? You mean he's come back and gone out again?"

"No, Madam. He's never been back."

The dread stirred again, and Mary knew that now it had her fast.

"Not since he went out with -- the gentleman?"

"Not since he went out with the gentleman."

"But who the gentleman?" Mary gasped out, with the sharp note of some one trying to be heard through a confusion of meaningless noises.

"That I couldn't say, Madam." Trimmle, standing there by the lamp, seemed suddenly to grow less round and rosy, as though *eclipsed* by the same creeping shade of apprehension.

"But the kitchen-maid knows -- wasn't it the kitchen-maid who let him in?"

"She doesn't know either, Madam, for he wrote his name on a folded paper."

Mary, through her agitation, was aware that they were both designating the unknown visitor by a vague pronoun, instead

Luncheon - *A formal lunch*
Lurking - *A hideout*
Aloof - *Detached*
Intangible - *Vague, unclear*
Propinquity - *Proximity*
Quavering - *To tremble with fear*
Dread - *To fear greatly*

of the conventional formula which, till then, had kept their allusions within the bounds of custom. And at the same moment her mind caught at the suggestion of the folded paper.

"But he must have a name! Where is the paper?"

She moved to the desk, and began to turn over the scattered documents that littered it. The first that caught her eye was an unfinished letter in her husband's hand, with his pen lying across it, as though dropped there at a sudden summons.

"My dear Parvis," -- who was Parvis? --"I have just received your letter announcing Elwell's death, and while I suppose there is now no farther risk of trouble, it might be safer --"

She tossed the sheet aside, and continued her search; but no folded paper was discoverable among the letters and pages of manuscript which had been swept together in a promiscuous heap, as if by a hurried or a startled gesture.

"But the kitchen-maid him. Send her here," she commanded, wondering at her dullness in not thinking sooner of so simple a solution.

Trimmle, at the behest, vanished in a flash, as if thankful to be out of the room, and when she reappeared, conducting the agitated underling, Mary had regained her self-possession, and had her questions pat.

The gentleman was a stranger, yes -- that she understood. But what had he said? And, above all, what had he looked like? The first question was easily enough answered, for the disconcerting reason that he had said so little -- had merely asked for Mr. Boyne, and, scribbling something on a bit of paper, had requested that it should at once be carried in to him.

"Then you don't know what he wrote? You're not sure it his name?"

The kitchen-maid was not sure, but supposed it was, since he had written it in answer to her inquiry as to whom she should announce.

"And when you carried the paper in to Mr. Boyne, what did he say?"

The kitchen-maid did not think that Mr. Boyne had said anything, but she could not be sure, for just as she had handed him the paper and he was opening it, she had become aware that the visitor had followed her into the library, and she had slipped out, leaving the two gentlemen together.

Conventional - *Adhering to accepted standards*
Allusions - *A passing reference*
Littered - *Scattered about*
Promiscuous - *Careless, haphazard*
Behest - *A to write hastily*
Disconcerting - *Disturbing scattered about*
Scribbling - *To write hastily*

"But then, if you left them in the library, how do you know that they went out of the house?"

This question plunged the witness into momentary inarticulateness, from which she was rescued by Trimmle, who, by means of ingenious circumlocutions, elicited the statement that before she could cross the hall to the back passage she had heard the gentlemen behind her, and had seen them go out of the front door together.

"Then, if you saw the gentleman twice, you must be able to tell me what he looked like."

But with this final challenge to her powers of expression it became clear that the limit of the kitchen-maid's endurance had been reached. The obligation of going to the front door to "show in" a visitor was in itself so subversive of the fundamental order of things that it had thrown her faculties into hopeless disarray, and she could only stammer out, after various panting efforts at evocation, "His hat, mum, was different-like, as you might say --"

"Different? How different?" Mary flashed out at her, her own mind, in the same instant, leaping back to an image left on it that morning, but temporarily lost under layers of subsequent impressions.

"His hat had a wide brim, you mean? and his face was pale -- a youngish face?" Mary pressed her, with a white-lipped intensity of interrogation. But if the kitchen-maid found any adequate answer to this challenge, it was swept away for her listener down the rushing current of her own convictions. The stranger -- the stranger in the garden! Why had Mary not thought of him before? She needed no one now to tell her that it was he who had called for her husband and gone away with him. But who was he, and why had Boyne obeyed his call?

IV

It leaped out at her suddenly, like a grin out of the dark, that they had often called England so little --"such a confoundedly hard place to get lost in."

That had been her husband's phrase. And now, with the whole machinery of official investigation sweeping its flash-lights from

Momentary - Temporary
Inarticulateness *- Unable to express oneself*
Circumlocutions - *An indirect expression*
Elicited *- To bring out evoke*
Obligation *- A binding promise*
Disarray *- Confusion*
Confoundedly - *Damned, Hopeless*

shore to shore, and across the dividing straits; now, with Boyne's name blazing from the walls of every town and village, his portrait (how that wrung her!) hawked up and down the country like the image of a hunted criminal; now the little compact, populous island, so policed, surveyed, and administered, revealed itself as a Sphinx-like guardian of abysmal mysteries, staring back into his wife's anguished eyes as if with the malicious joy of knowing something they would never know!

In the fortnight since Boyne's disappearance there had been no word of him, no trace of his movements. Even the usual misleading reports that raise expectancy in tortured bosoms had been few and fleeting. No one but the bewildered kitchen-maid had seen him leave the house, and no one else had seen "the gentleman" who accompanied him. All inquiries in the neighborhood failed to elicit the memory of a stranger's presence that day in the neighborhood of Lyng. And no one had met Edward Boyne, either alone or in company, in any of the neighbouring villages, or on the road across the downs, or at either of the local railway-stations. The sunny English noon had swallowed him as completely as if he had gone out into Cimmerian night.

Mary, while every external means of investigation was working at its highest pressure, had ransacked her husband's papers for any trace of antecedent complications, of entanglements or obligations unknown to her, that might throw a faint ray into the darkness. But if any such had existed in the background of Boyne's life, they had disappeared as completely as the slip of paper on which the visitor had written his name. There remained no possible thread of guidance except -- if it were indeed an exception -- the letter which Boyne had apparently been in the act of writing when he received his mysterious summons. That letter, read and reread by his wife, and submitted by her to the police, yielded little enough for conjecture to feed on.

"I have just heard of Elwell's death, and while I suppose there is now no farther risk of trouble, it might be safer --" That was all. The "risk of trouble" was easily explained by the newspaper clipping which had apprised Mary of the suit brought against her husband by one of his associates in the Blue Star enterprise. The only new information conveyed in the letter was the fact of its showing Boyne, when he wrote it, to be still apprehensive of the results of the suit, though he had assured his wife that it had been

---

Abysmal - *Very great*
Malicious - *Vicious*
Antecedent - *Pre-existent, presursor*
Entanglements - *Sexual involvements con*
Summons - *Commands*

withdrawn, and though the letter itself declared that the plaintiff was dead. It took several weeks of exhaustive cabling to fix the identity of the "Parvis" to whom the fragmentary communication was addressed, but even after these inquiries had shown him to be a Waukesha lawyer, no new facts concerning the Elwell suit were elicited. He appeared to have had no direct concern in it, but to have been conversant with the facts merely as an acquaintance, and possible intermediary; and he declared himself unable to divine with what object Boyne intended to seek his assistance.

This negative information, sole fruit of the first fortnight's feverish search, was not increased by a jot during the slow weeks that followed. Mary knew that the investigations were still being carried on, but she had a vague sense of their gradually slackening, as the actual march of time seemed to slacken. It was as though the days, flying horror-struck from the shrouded image of the one inscrutable day, gained assurance as the distance lengthened, till at last they fell back into their normal gait. And so with the human imaginations at work on the dark event. No doubt it occupied them still, but week by week and hour by hour it grew less absorbing, took up less space, was slowly but inevitably crowded out of the foreground of consciousness by the new problems perpetually bubbling up from the vaporous caldron of human experience.

Even Mary Boyne's consciousness gradually felt the same lowering of velocity. It still swayed with the incessant oscillations of conjecture; but they were slower, more rhythmical in their beat. There were moments of overwhelming lassitude when, like the victim of some poison which leaves the brain clear, but holds the body motionless, she saw herself domesticated with the Horror, accepting its perpetual presence as one of the fixed conditions of life.

These moments lengthened into hours and days, till she passed into a phase of stolid acquiescence. She watched the familiar routine of life with the incurious eye of a savage on whom the meaningless processes of civilization make but the faintest impression. She had come to regard herself as part of the routine, a spoke of the wheel, revolving with its motion; she felt almost like the furniture of the room in which she sat, an insensate object to be dusted and pushed about with the chairs and tables. And this deepening apathy held her fast at Lyng, in spite of the urgent entreaties of friends

Elicited - *Evoked*
Plaintiff -*A person who brings suit in a court*
Slackening - *Become slower*
Inscrutable - *Incapable of careful study*
Inevitably - *Insensate foolish without sense*
Lassitude - *Weariness*

and the usual medical recommendation of "change." Her friends supposed that her refusal to move was inspired by the belief that her husband would one day return to the spot from which he had vanished, and a beautiful legend grew up about this imaginary state of waiting. But in reality she had no such belief: the depths of anguish inclosing her were no longer lighted by flashes of hope. She was sure that Boyne would never come back, that he had gone out of her sight as completely as if Death itself had waited that day on the threshold. She had even renounced, one by one, the various theories as to his disappearance which had been advanced by the press, the police, and her own agonized imagination. In sheer lassitude her mind turned from these alternatives of horror, and sank back into the blank fact that he was gone.

No, she would never know what had become of him -- no one would ever know. But the house ; the library in which she spent her long, lonely evenings knew. For it was here that the last scene had been enacted, here that the stranger had come, and spoken the word which had caused Boyne to rise and follow him. The floor she trod had felt his tread; the books on the shelves had seen his face; and there were moments when the intense consciousness of the old, dusky walls seemed about to break out into some *audible revelation* of their secret. But the revelation never came, and she knew it would never come. Lyng was not one of the garrulous old houses that betray the secrets *entrusted* to them. Its very legend proved that it had always been the mute accomplice, the *incorruptible* custodian of the mysteries it had surprised. And Mary Boyne, sitting face to face with its portentous silence, felt the *futility* of seeking to break it by any human means.

V

Garrulous -
Talkative
Futility - Lack of purpose
Audible - *Capable of being heard*
Revelation -
Divulgation
Incorruptible -
Upright
Entrusted - *To put in chage*

"I don't say it straight, yet don't say it straight. It was business."

Mary, at the words, lifted her head with a start, and looked *intently* at the speaker.

When, half an hour before, a card with "Mr. Parvis" on it had been brought up to her, she had been immediately aware that the name had been a part of her consciousness ever since she had read it at the head of Boyne's unfinished letter. In the library she had found awaiting her a small neutral-tinted man with a bald head and gold eye-glasses, and it sent a strange tremor through her to know that this was the person to whom her husband's last known thought had been directed.

Parvis, civilly, but without vain preamble, -- in the manner of a man who has his watch in his hand, -- had set forth the object of his visit. He had "run over" to England on business, and finding himself in the neighbourhood of Dorchester, had not wished to leave it without paying his respects to Mrs. Boyne; without asking her, if the occasion offered, what she meant to do about Bob Elwell's family.

The words touched the spring of some obscure dread in Mary's bosom. Did her visitor, after all, know what Boyne had meant by his unfinished phrase? She asked for an elucidation of his question, and noticed at once that he seemed surprised at her continued ignorance of the subject. Was it possible that she really knew as little as she said?

"I know nothing -- you must tell me," she faltered out; and her visitor thereupon proceeded to unfold his story. It threw, even to her confused perceptions, and imperfectly *initiated* vision, a lurid glare on the whole hazy episode of the Blue Star Mine. Her husband had made his money in that brilliant speculation at the cost of "getting ahead" of some one less alert to seize the chance; the victim of his *ingenuity* was young Robert Elwell, who had "put him on" to the Blue Star scheme.

Parvis, at Mary's first *startled* cry, had thrown her a sobering glance through his *impartial* glasses. "Bob Elwell wasn't smart enough, that's all; if he had been, he might have turned round and served Boyne the same way. It's the kind of thing that happens every day in business. I guess it's what the scientists call the survival of the fittest," said Mr. Parvis, evidently pleased with the aptness of his *analogy*.

Mary felt a physical *shrinking* from the next question she tried to frame; it was as though the words on her lips had a taste that *nauseated* her.

"But then -- you accuse my husband of doing something dishonourable?"

Mr. Parvis surveyed the question dispassionately. "Oh, no, I don't. I don't even say it wasn't straight." He glanced up and down the long lines of books, as if one of them might have supplied him with the definition he sought. "I don't say it straight,

Ingenuity - *Cleverness*
Startled - *Very surprised*
Analogy - *Similarity*
Nauseated - *To feel sick*

and yet I don't say it straight. It was business." After all, no definition in his category could be more *comprehensive* than that.

Mary sat staring at him with a look of terror. He seemed to her like the indifferent, implacable emissary of some dark, formless power.

"But Mr. Elwell's lawyers apparently did not take your view, since I suppose the suit was withdrawn by their advice."

"Oh, yes, they knew he hadn't a leg to stand on, technically. It was when they advised him to withdraw the suit that he got desperate. You see, he'd borrowed most of the money he lost in the Blue Star, and he was up a tree. That's why he shot himself when they told him he had no show."

The horror was sweeping over Mary in great, *deafening* waves.

"He shot himself? He killed himself because of? "

"Well, he didn't kill himself, exactly. He dragged on two months before he died." Parvis emitted the statement as unemotionally as a gramophone grinding out its "record."

"You mean that he tried to kill himself, and failed? And tried again?"

"Oh, he didn't have to try again," said Parvis, grimly.

They sat opposite each other in silence, he swinging his eyeglass thoughtfully about his finger, she, motionless, her arms stretched along her knees in an attitude of rigid tension. "But if you knew all this," she began at length, hardly able to force her voice above a whisper, "how is it that when I wrote you at the time of my husband's disappearance you said you didn't understand his letter?"

Parvis received this without perceptible *discomfiture*. "Why, I didn't understand it -- strictly speaking. And it wasn't the time to talk about it, if I had. The Elwell business was settled when the suit was withdrawn. Nothing I could have told you would have helped you to find your husband."

Mary continued to *scrutinize* him. "Then why are you telling me now?"

Still Parvis did not hesitate. "Well, to begin with, I supposed you knew more than you appear to -- I mean about the circumstances of Elwell's death. And then people are talking of it now; the whole matter's been *raked* up again. And I thought, if you didn't know, you ought to."

Comprehensive - *Extensive*
Discomfiture - *Confusion*
Serutinize - *To examine in detail*
Raked - *To gather*

She remained silent, and he continued: "You see, it's only come out lately what a bad state Elwell's affairs were in. His wife's a proud woman, and she fought on as long as she could, going out to work, and taking sewing at home, when she got too sick-something with the heart, I believe. But she had his bedridden mother to look after, and the children, and she broke down under it, and finally had to ask for help. That attracted attention to the case, and the papers took it up, and a subscription was started. Everybody out there liked Bob Elwell, and most of the prominent names in the place are down on the list, and people began to wonder why --"

Parvis broke off to fumble in an inner pocket. "Here," he continued, "here's an account of the whole thing from the 'Sentinel' -- a little *sensational*, of course. But I guess you'd better look it over."

He held out a newspaper to Mary, who unfolded it slowly, remembering, as she did so, the evening when, in that same room, the perusal of a clipping from the "Sentinel" had first shaken the depths of her security.

As she opened the paper, her eyes, shrinking from the glaring head-lines, "Widow of Boyne's Victim Forced to Appeal for Aid," ran down the column of text to two portraits *inserted* in it. The first was her husband's, taken from a photograph made the year they had come to England. It was the picture of him that she liked best, the one that stood on the writing-table up-stairs in her bedroom. As the eyes in the photograph met hers, she felt it would be impossible to read what was said of him, and closed her lids with the sharpness of the pain.

"I thought if you felt disposed to put your name down --" she heard Parvis continue.

She opened her eyes with an effort, and they fell on the other portrait. It was that of a youngish man, slightly built, in rough clothes, with features somewhat blurred by the shadow of a *projecting* hat-brim. Where had she seen that outline before? She stared at it confusedly, her heart hammering in her throat and ears. Then she gave a cry.

"This is the man -- the man who came for my husband!"

She heard Parvis start to his feet, and was dimly aware that she had slipped backward into the corner of the sofa, and that he was bending above her in alarm. With an intense effort she

Projecting - *Proposing planning*
Sensational - *Exciting*
Subscription - *A payment for a magazine*
Inserted - *To put or between*

straightened herself, and reached out for the paper, which she had dropped.

"It's the man! I should know him anywhere!" she cried in a voice that sounded in her own ears like a scream.

Parvis's voice seemed to come to her from far off, down endless, fog-muffled windings.

"Mrs. Boyne, you're not very well. Shall I call somebody? Shall I get a glass of water?"

"No, no, no!" She threw herself toward him, her hand *frantically* clenching the newspaper. "I tell you, it's the man! I him! He spoke to me in the garden!"

Parvis took the journal from her, directing his glasses to the portrait. "It can't be, Mrs. Boyne. It's Robert Elwell."

"Robert Elwell?" Her white stare seemed to travel into space. "Then it was Robert Elwell who came for him."

"Came for Boyne? The day he went away?" Parvis's voice dropped as hers rose. He bent over, laying a *fraternal* hand on her, as if to coax her gently back into her seat. "Why, Elwell was dead! Don't you remember?"

Mary sat with her eyes fixed on the picture, unconscious of what he was saying.

"Don't you remember Boyne's unfinished letter to me -- the one you found on his desk that day? It was written just after he'd heard of Elwell's death." She noticed an odd shake in Parvis's unemotional voice. "Surely you remember that!" he urged her.

Yes, she remembered: that was the *profoundest* horror of it. Elwell had died the day before her husband's disappearance; and this was Elwell's portrait; and it was the portrait of the man who had spoken to her in the garden. She lifted her head and looked slowly about the library. The library could have borne witness that it was also the portrait of the man who had come in that day to call Boyne from his unfinished letter. Through the misty *surgings* of her brain she heard the faint boom of halfforgotten words -- words spoken by Alida Stair on the lawn at Pangbourne before Boyne and his wife had ever seen the house at Lyng, or had imagined that they might one day live there.

"This was the man who spoke to me," she repeated.

She looked again at Parvis. He was trying to conceal his disturbance under what he imagined to be an expression of *indulgent commiseration*; but the edges of his lips were blue. "He

Projecting - *Directing devised*
Frantically - *Desperately*
Fraternal - *Brotherly*
Profoundes - *Deep, sagacious*

thinks me mad; but I'm not mad," she reflected; and suddenly there flashed upon her a way of justifying her strange affirmation.

She sat quiet, controlling the quiver of her lips, and waiting till she could trust her voice to keep its habitual level; then she said, looking straight at Parvis: "Will you answer me one question, please? When was it that Robert Elwell tried to kill himself?"

"When -- when?" Parvis stammered.

"Yes; the date. Please try to remember."

She saw that he was growing still more afraid of her. "I have a reason," she insisted gently.

"Yes, yes. Only I can't remember. About two months before, I should say."

"I want the date," she repeated.

Parvis picked up the newspaper. "We might see here," he said, still humouring her. He ran his eyes down the page. "Here it is. Last October -- the --"

She caught the words from him. "The 20th, wasn't it?" With a sharp look at her, he verified. "Yes, the 20th. Then you know?"

"I know now." Her white stare continued to travel past him. "Sunday, the 20th -- that was the day he came first."

Parvis's voice was almost *inaudible*. "Came first?"

"Yes." "You saw him twice, then?"

"Yes, twice." She breathed it at him with dilated eyes. "He came first on the 20th of October. I remember the date because it was the day we went up Meldon Steep for the first time." She felt a faint gasp of inward laughter at the thought that but for that she might have forgotten.

Parvis continued to *scrutinise* her, as if trying to intercept her gaze.

"We saw him from the roof," she went on. "He came down the limeavenue toward the house. He was dressed just as he is in that picture. My husband saw him first. He was frightened, and ran down ahead of me; but there was no one there. He had vanished."

"Elwell had vanished?" Parvis faltered.

"Yes." Their two whispers seemed to grope for each other. "I couldn't think what had happened. I see now. He to come then; but he wasn't dead enough -- he couldn't reach us. He had to wait for two months; and then he came back again -- and Ned went with him."

Surging - *Forward movement*
Indulgent - *Tolerant*
Commiseration - *Expressing sorrow sympathise*
Inaudible - *Not lout enough to be heard*

Greatest Ghost Stories

She nodded at Parvis with the look of **triumph** of a child who has successfully worked out a difficult puzzle. But suddenly she lifted her hands with a desperate gesture, pressing them to her bursting temples.

"Oh, my God! I sent him to Ned -- I told him where to go! I sent him to this room!" she screamed out.

She felt the walls of the room rush toward her, like inward falling ruins; and she heard Parvis, a long way off, as if through the ruins, crying to her, and struggling to get at her. But she was numb to his touch, she did not know what he was saying. Through the **tumult** she heard but one clear note, the voice of Alida Stair, speaking on the lawn at Pangbourne.

"You won't know till afterward," it said. "You won't know till long, long afterward."

Food For Thought

Mary recalls Parvis' visit and his explanation about the bad business deal at the Blue Star Mine by her husband, Ned that destroyed the life of a man called Elwell. When she sees the picture of Elwell, she realises the identity of the strange searching for Ned. Do you think Mary was right in her assumption that the ghost of Elwell had taken her husband away? Give reasons for your answer.

Nodded - *To make a slight, downward bending movement*
Temples - *Victory*
Tumult - *Uproar, violent, noisy sound*

Greatest Ghost Stories

An Understanding

Q. 1. How does the story begin? What happened for the past six months that lead to the disappearance of Mary's husband, Ned?
Ans. _____
_____
_____
_____
_____

Q. 2. The Boyne's were nouveau riche because of a business deal made by Ned and were looking for a place to pursue their dream of a life of leisure. Who was Alida Stair and why did she suggest Lyng in Dorsetshire as the ideal place?
Ans. _____
_____
_____
_____
_____

Q. 3. Why was Ned worried and withdrawn from others before disappearing mysteriously? What was the newspaper clipping all about and why did Mary question Ned about it, though she never took interest in his business deals?
Ans. _____
_____
_____
_____

Q. 4. Relate the incident briefly that occurred the day when a stranger approached and inquired about Mary's husband.
Ans. _____
_____
_____
_____
_____

Sir Edmund Orme
Henry James

THe statement appears to have been written, though the fragment is undated, long after the death of his wife, whom I take to have been one of the persons referred to. There is, however, nothing in the strange story to establish this point, which is, perhaps, not of importance. When I took possession of his effects I found these pages, in a locked drawer, among papers relating to the unfortunate lady's too brief career (she died in childbirth a year after her marriage), letters, memoranda, accounts, faded photographs, cards of invitation. That is the only connection I can point to, and you may easily and will probably say that the tale is too extravagant to have had a demonstrable origin. I cannot, I admit, vouch for his having intended it as a report of real occurrence -- I can only vouch for his general veracity. In any case it was written for himself, not for others. I offer it to others -- having full option -- precisely because it is so singular. Let them, in respect to the form of the thing, bear in mind that it was written quite for himself. I have altered nothing but the names.

*

If there's a story in the matter I recognise the exact moment at which it began. This was on a soft, still Sunday noon in November, just after church, on the sunny Parade. Brighton was full of people; it was the height of the season, and the day was even more respectable than lovely -- which helped to account for the multitude of walkers. The blue sea itself was decorous; it seemed to doze, with a gentle snore (if that decorum), as if nature were preaching a sermon. After writing letters all the morning, I had come out to take a look at it before luncheon. I was leaning over the rail which separates the King's Road from the beach, and I think I was smoking a cigarette, when I became conscious of an intended joke in the shape of a light walking-stick laid across my shoulders. The idea, I found, had been thrown off by Teddy Bostwick, of the Rifles, and was intended as a contribution to talk. Our talk came off as we strolled together -- he always took

---

Fragment - *A very small piece or bit of something*
Vouch - *Certify, guarantee*
Veracity - *Honesty, integrity*
Multitude - *A great number*
Snore - *To breathe during sleep with a harsh sound*

your arm to show you he forgave your **obtuseness** about his humour -- and looked at the people, and bowed to some of them, and wondered who others were, and differed in opinion as to the prettiness of the girls. About Charlotte Marden we agreed, however, as we saw her coming toward us with her mother; and there surely could have been no one who wouldn't have agreed with us. The Brighton air, of old, used to make plain girls pretty and pretty girls prettier still -- I don't know whether it works the spell now. The place, at any rate, was rare for complexions, and Miss Marden's was one that made people turn round. It made stop, heaven knows -- at least, it was one of the things, for we already knew the ladies.

We turned with them, we joined them, we went where they were going. They were only going to the end and back -- they had just come out of church. It was another manifestation of Teddy's humour that he got immediate **possession** of Charlotte, leaving me to walk with her mother. However, I was not unhappy; the girl was before me and I had her to talk about. We *prolonged* our walk, Mrs Marden kept me, and presently she said she was tired and must sit down. We found a place on a sheltered bench -- we gossiped as the people passed. It had already struck me, in this pair, that the resemblance between the mother and the daughter was wonderful even among such **resemblances** -- the more so that it took so little account of a difference of nature. One often hears mature mothers spoken of as warnings -- signposts, more or less discouraging, of the way daughters may go. But there was nothing deterrent in the idea that Charlotte, at fifty-five, should be as beautiful, even though it were conditioned on her being as pale and preoccupied, as Mrs Marden. At twenty-two she had a kind of rosy blankness and she was admirably handsome. Her head had the charming shape of her mother's, and her features the same fine order. Then there were looks and movements and tones (moments when you could scarcely say whether it were aspect or sound), which, between the two personalities, were a reflection, a recall.

These ladies had a small fortune and a cheerful little house at Brighton, full of portraits and **tokens** and trophies (stuffed animals on the top of bookcases, and sallow, varnished fish under glass), to which Mrs Marden professed herself attached by pious memories. Her husband had been 'ordered' there in ill-health, to spend the last years of his life,

Obtuseness - *Not quick, or alert*
Possession - *Under control, owned*
Prolonged - *Extend*
Resemblances - *Similarity in appearance*
Tokens - *Momentous, souvenirs*

and she had already mentioned to me that it was a place in which she felt herself still under the protection of his goodness. His goodness appeared to have been great, and she sometimes had the air of defending it against mysterious *imputations*. Some sense of protection, of an influence invoked and cherished, was evidently necessary to her; she had a dim *wistfulness*, a longing for security. She wanted friends and she had a good many. She was kind to me on our first meeting, and I never suspected her of the vulgar purpose of 'making up' to me -- a suspicion, of course, unduly frequent in conceited young men. It never struck me that she wanted me for her daughter, nor yet, like some unnatural mammas, for herself. It was as if they had had a common deep, shy need and had been ready to say: 'Oh, be friendly to us and be trustful! Don't be afraid, you won't be expected to marry us.' "Of course there's something about mamma; that's really what makes her such a dear!" Charlotte said to me, *confidentially*, at an early stage of our *acquaintance*. She worshipped her mother's appearance. It was the only thing she was vain of; she accepted the raised eyebrows as a charming ultimate fact. "She looks as if she were waiting for the doctor, dear mamma," she said on another occasion. "Perhaps the doctor; do you think you are?" It appeared in the event that I had some healing power. At any rate when I learned, for she once dropped the remark, that Mrs Marden also thought there was something 'awfully strange' about Charlotte, the relation between the two ladies became extremely interesting. It was happy enough, at bottom; each had the other so much on her mind.

On the Parade the stream of strollers held its course, and Charlotte presently went by with Teddy Bostwick. She smiled and nodded and continued, but when she came back she stopped and spoke to us. Captain Bostwick positively declined to go in, he said the occasion was too jolly: might they therefore take another turn? Her mother dropped a "Do as you like", and the girl gave me an impertinent smile over her shoulder as they *quitted* us. Teddy looked at me with his glass in one eye; but I didn't mind that; it was only of Miss Marden I was thinking as I observed to my companion, laughing:

"She's a bit of a coquette, you know."

"Don't say that -- don't say that!" Mrs Marden *murmured*.

Imputations - *Accusations*
Wistfulness - *Melancholies*
Confidentially - *Secretly, privately*
Acquaintance - *A person with whom one has been in contact*
Quitted - *To leave resign*
Murmured - *To speak in a low tone*

"The nicest girls always are -- just a little," I was magnanimous enough to plead.

"Then why are they always punished?"

The *intensity* of the question startled me -- it had come out in such a vivid flash. Therefore I had to think a moment before I inquired: "What do you know about it?"

"I was a bad girl myself."

"And were you punished?"

"I carry it through life," said Mrs Marden, looking away from me. "Ah!" she suddenly panted, in the next breath, rising to her feet and staring at her daughter, who had reappeared again with Captain Bostwick. She stood a few seconds, with the *queerest* expression in her face; then she sank upon the seat again and I saw that she had blushed crimson. Charlotte, who had observed her movement, came straight up to her and, taking her hand with quick tenderness, seated herself on the other side of her. The girl had turned *pale* -- she gave her mother a fixed, frightened look. Mrs Marden, who had had some shock which escaped our detection, recovered herself; that is she sat quiet and inexpressive, gazing at the indifferent crowd, the sunny air, the *slumbering* sea. My eye happened to fall, however, on the interlocked hands of the two ladies, and I quickly guessed that the grasp of the elder one was violent. Bostwick stood before them, wondering what was the matter and asking me from his little vacant disk if knew; which led Charlotte to say to him after a moment, with a certain *irritation*:

"Don't stand there that way, Captain Bostwick; go away -- go away."

I got up at this, hoping that Mrs Marden wasn't ill; but she immediately begged that we would go away, that we would particularly stay and that we would presently come home to lunch. She drew me down beside her and for a moment I felt her hand pressing my arm in a way that might have been an *involuntary betrayal* of distress and might have been a private signal. What she might have wished to point out to me I couldn't divine: perhaps she had seen somebody or something abnormal in the crowd. She explained to us in a few minutes that she was all right; that she was only liable to *palpitations* -- they came as quickly as they went. It was time to move, and we moved. The incident was felt to be closed.

Intensity - *Strength, Concentration*
Vivid - *Very clear*
Queerest - *Very strange*
Pale - *Faint, feeble*
Involuntary - *Uncontrolled*
Betrayal - *Trashiness, disloyalty*
Palpitations - *Abnormal or violent beating of the heart*

Bostwick and I lunched with our sociable friends, and when I walked away with him he declared that he had never seen such dear kind creatures.

Mrs Marden had made us promise to come back the next day to tea, and had **exhorted** us in general to come as often as we could. Yet the next day, when at five o'clock I knocked at the door of the pretty house, it was to learn that the ladies had gone up to town. They had left a message for us with the butler: he was to say that they had suddenly been called -- were very sorry. They would be absent a few days. This was all I could extract from the *dumb* domestic. I went again three days later, but they were still away; and it was not till the end of a week that I got a note from Mrs Marden, saying 'We are back; do come and forgive us.' It was on this occasion, I remember (the occasion of my going just after getting the note), that she told me she had intuitions. I don't know how many people there were in England at that time in that *predicament*, but there were very few who would have mentioned it; so that the announcement struck me as original, especially as her point was that some of these uncanny *promptings* were connected with me. There were other people present -- idle Brighton folk, old women with frightened eyes and irrelevant interjections -- and I had but a few minutes' talk with Charlotte; but the day after this I met them both at dinner and had the satisfaction of sitting next to Miss Marden. I recall that hour as the hour on which it first completely came over me that she was a beautiful, liberal creature. I had seen her personality in patches and *gleams*, like a song sung in snatches, but now it was before me in a large rosy glow, as if it had been a full volume of sound -- I heard the whole of the air. It was sweet, fresh music -- I was often to hum it over.

After dinner I had a few words with Mrs Marden; it was at the moment, late in the evening, when tea was handed about. A servant passed near us with a tray, I asked her if she would have a cup, and, on her *assenting*, took one and handed it to her. She put out her hand for it and I gave it to her, safely as I supposed; but as she was in the act of receiving it she started and faltered, so that the cup and saucer dropped with a crash of porcelain and without, on the part of my *interlocutress*, the usual woman's movement to save her dress. I stooped to pick up the fragments and when I raised myself Mrs Marden was looking across the room at her daughter, who looked back at

Exhorted - *Urged, advised*
Predicament - *Unpleasant or puzzling situation*
Promptings - *Serving to suggest/remind*
Gleams - *Dim*

her smiling, but with an anxious light in her eyes. 'Dear mamma, what on earth the matter with you?' the silent question seemed to say. Mrs Marden coloured, just as she had done after her strange movement on the Parade the other week, and I was therefore surprised when she said to me with unexpected assurance: "You should really have a steadier hand!" I had begun to *stammer* a defence of my hand when I became aware that she had fixed her eyes upon me with an intense appeal. It was *ambiguous* at first and only added to my confusion; then suddenly I understood, as plainly as if she had murmured 'Make believe it was you -- make believe it was you.' The servant came back to take the morsels of the cup and wipe up the spilt tea, and while I was in the midst of making believe Mrs Marden abruptly brushed away from me and from her daughter's attention and went into another room. I noticed that she gave no heed to the state of her dress.

I saw nothing more of either of them that evening, but the next morning, in the King's Road, I met Miss Marden with a roll of music in her muff. She told me she had been a little way alone, to practice duets with a friend, and I asked her if she would go a little way further in company. She gave me leave to attend her to her door, and as we stood before it I inquired if I might go in. "No, not to-day -- I don't want you," she said, *candidly*, though not roughly; while the words caused me to direct a wistful, disconcerted gaze at one of the windows of the house. It fell upon the white face of Mrs Marden, who was looking out at us from the drawing-room. She stood there long enough for me to see that it she and not an *apparition*, as I had thought for a second, and then she vanished before her daughter had observed her. The girl, during our walk, had said nothing about her. As I had been told they didn't want me I left them alone a little, after which circumstances *supervened* that kept us still longer apart. I finally went up to London, and while there I received a pressing invitation to come immediately down to Tranton, a pretty old place in Sussex belonging to a couple whose acquaintance I had lately made.

I went to Tranton from town, and on arriving found the Mardens, with a dozen other people, in the house. The first thing Mrs Marden said was: "Will you forgive me?" and when I asked what I had to forgive she answered: "My throwing my tea over you." I replied that it had gone over herself; whereupon she said: "At any rate I was very rude; but some

Stammer - *To speak in a hesitant way, a speech disorder*
Ambiguous - *Vague, obscure*
Candidly - *Frankly*
Apparition - *Ghost*
Supervened - *Followed closely, ensured*

day I think you'll understand, and then you'll make ***allowances*** for me." The first day I was there she dropped two or three of these references (she had already indulged in more than one), to the mystic ***initiation*** that was in store for me; so that I began, as the phrase is, to chaff her about it, to say I would rather it were less wonderful and take it out at once. She answered that when it should come to me I would have to take it out -- there would be little enough option. That it come was privately clear to her, a deep ***presentiment***, which was the only reason she had ever mentioned the matter. Didn't I remember she had told me she had intuitions? From the first time of her seeing me she had been sure there were things I should not escape knowing. Meanwhile there was nothing to do but wait and keep cool, not to be precipitate. She particularly wished not to be any more nervous than she was. And I was above all not to be nervous myself -- one got used to everything. I declared that though I couldn't make out what she was talking about I was terribly frightened; the absence of a clue gave such a range to one's imagination. I exaggerated on purpose; for if Mrs Marden was ***mystifying*** I can scarcely say she was alarming. I couldn't imagine what she meant, but I wondered more than I shuddered. I might have said to myself that she was a little wrong in the upper story; but that never occurred to me. She struck me as hopelessly right.

There were other girls in the house, but Charlotte Marden was the most charming; which was so generally felt to be the case that she really interfered with the slaughter of ground game. There were two or three men, and I was of the number, who actually preferred her to the society of the beaters. In short she was recognised as a form of sport superior and exquisite. She was kind to all of us -- she made us go out late and come in early. I don't know whether she flirted, but several other members of the party thought did. Indeed, as regards himself, Teddy Bostwick, who had come over from Brighton, was visibly sure.

The third day I was at Tranton was a Sunday, and there was a very pretty walk to morning service over the fields. It was grey, windless weather, and the bell of the little old church that nestled in the hollow of the Sussex down sounded near and domestic. We were a ***straggling*** procession, in the mild damp air (which, as always at that season, gave one the feeling that after the trees were bare there was more of it -- a

Allowances - *Stipend*
Initiation - *Originate*
Presentiment - *Premonition, a sense of something about to happen*
Mystifying - *Perplexing*
Straggling - *To stray, wander*

larger sky), and I managed to fall a good way behind with Miss Marden. I remember entertaining, as we moved together over the turf, a strong impulse to say something intensely personal, something violent and important -- important for, such as that I had never seen her so lovely, or that that particular moment was the sweetest of my life. But always, in youth, such words have been on the lips many times before they are spoken; and I had the sense, not that I didn't know her well enough (I cared little for that), but that she didn't know well enough. In the church, where there were old Tranton tombs and brasses, the big Tranton pew was full. Several of us were scattered, and I found a seat for Miss Marden, and another for myself beside it, at a distance from her mother and from most of our friends. There were two or three decent *rustics* on the bench, who moved in further to make room for us, and I took my place first, to cut off my companion from our neighbours. After she was seated there was still a space left, which remained empty till service was about half over.

This at least was the moment at which I became aware that another person had entered and had taken the seat. When I noticed him he had apparently been for some minutes in the pew, for he had settled himself and put down his hat beside him, and, with his hands crossed on the nob of his cane, was gazing before him at the altar. He was a pale young man in black, with the air of a gentleman. I was slightly startled on *perceiving* him, for Miss Marden had not attracted my attention to his entrance by moving to make room for him. After a few minutes, observing that he had no prayer-book, I reached across my neighbour and placed mine before him, on the ledge of the pew; a manœuvre the motive of which was not unconnected with the possibility that, in my own *destitution*, Miss Marden would give me one side of velvet volume to hold. The pretext, however, was destined to fail for at the moment I offered him the book the intruder -- whose *intrusion* I had so condoned -- rose from his place without thanking me, stepped noiselessly out of the pew (it had no door), and, so discreetly as to attract no attention, passed down the centre of the church. A few minutes had sufficed for his devotions. His behaviour was unbecoming, his early departure even more than his late arrival; but he managed so quietly that we were not *incommoded*, and I perceived, on turning a little to glance after him, that nobody was disturbed by his withdrawal. I

Rustics - *Uncouth, rude persons*
Perceiving - *Recognising, discerning*
Destitution - *Deprivation*
Intrusion - *An illegal act of entering*
Incommoded - *Disturbed troubled*

Greatest Ghost Stories

only noticed, and with surprise, that Mrs Marden had been so affected by it as to rise, *involuntarily*, an instant, in her place. She stared at him as he passed, but he passed very quickly, and she as quickly dropped down again, though not too soon to catch my eye across the church. Five minutes later I asked Miss Marden, in a low voice, if she would kindly pass me back my prayer-book -- I had waited to see if she would spontaneously perform the act. She *restored* this aid to devotion, but had been so far from troubling herself about it that she could say to me as she did so: "Why on earth did you put it there?" I was on the point of answering her when she dropped on her knees, and I held my tongue. I had only been going to say: 'To be decently civil.'

After the *benediction*, as we were leaving our places, I was slightly surprised, again, to see that Mrs Marden, instead of going out with her companions, had come up the aisle to join us, having apparently something to say to her daughter. She said it, but in an instant I observed that it was only a *pretext* -- her real business was with me. She pushed Charlotte forward and suddenly murmured to me: "Did you see him?"

"The gentleman who sat down here? How could I help seeing him?"

"Hush!" she said, with the intensest excitement; "don't to her -- don't tell her!" She slipped her hand into my arm, to keep me near her, to keep me, it seemed, away from her daughter. The precaution was unnecessary, for Teddy Bostwick had already taken possession of Miss Marden, and as they passed out of church in front of me I saw one of the other men close up on her other hand. It appeared to be considered that I had had my turn. Mrs Marden withdrew her hand from my arm as soon as we got out, but not before I felt that she had really needed the support. "Don't speak to any one -- don't tell any one!" she went on.

"I don't understand. Tell them what?"

"Why, that you saw him."

"Surely they saw him for themselves."

"Not one of them, not one of them." She spoke in a tone of such *passionate* decision that I *glanced* at her -- she was staring straight before her. But she felt the challenge of my eyes and she stopped short, in the old brown timber porch of the

Restored - *To bring back into existence*
Benediction - *An utterance of good wishes*
Pretext - *Excuse*
Passionate - *Ruled by intense emotion*
Glanced - *To look quickly or briefly*

Greatest Ghost Stories

church, with the others well in advance of us, and said, looking at me now and in a quite ***extraordinary*** manner: "You're the only person, the only person in the world."

"But, dear madam?"

"Oh me -- of course. That's my curse!" And with this she moved rapidly away from me to join the body of the party. I hovered on its outskirts on the way home, for I had food for ***rumination***. Whom had I seen and why was the apparition -- it rose before my mind's eye very vividly again -- invisible to the others? If an exception had been made for Mrs Marden, why did it constitute a curse, and why was I to share so questionable an advantage? This inquiry, carried on in my own locked breast, kept me doubtless silent enough during luncheon. After luncheon I went out on the old terrace to smoke a cigarette, but I had only taken a couple of turns when I perceived Mrs Marden's moulded mask at the window of one of the rooms which opened on the crooked flags. It reminded me of the same ***flitting*** presence at the window at Brighton the day I met Charlotte and walked home with her. But this time my ambiguous friend didn't vanish; she tapped on the pane and motioned me to come in. She was in a queer little apartment, one of the many reception-rooms of which the ground-floor at Tranton consisted; it was known as the Indian room and had a decoration ***vaguely*** Oriental -- bamboo ***lounges***, lacquered screens, lanterns with long fringes and strange idols in cabinets, objects not held to conduce to sociability. The place was little used, and when I went round to her we had it to ourselves. As soon as I entered she said to me: "Please tell me this; are you in love with my daughter?"

I hesitated a moment. "Before I answer your question will you kindly tell me what gives you the idea? I don't consider that I have been very forward."

Mrs Marden, ***contradicting*** me with her beautiful anxious eyes, gave me no satisfaction on the point I mentioned; she only went on ***strenuously***:

"Did you say nothing to her on the way to church?"

"What makes you think I said anything?"

"The fact that you saw him."

"Saw whom, dear Mrs Marden?"

"Oh, you know," she answered, gravely, even a little reproachfully, as if I were trying to humiliate her by making her phrase the unphraseable.

Rumination - *Ponder*
Lounges - *To pass time idly*
Flitting - *To move lightly and swiftly*
Vaguely - *Not clearly*
Contradicting - *To speak or declare against*

"Do you mean the gentleman who formed the subject of your strange statement in church -- the one who came into the pew?"

"You saw him, you saw him!" Mrs Marden **panted**, with a strange mixture of dismay and relief.

"Of course I saw him; and so did you."

"It didn't follow. Did you feel it to be inevitable?"

I was puzzled again. "***Inevitable***?"

"That you see him?"

"Certainly, since I'm not blind."

"You might have been; every one else is." I was wonderfully at sea, and I frankly confessed it to my ***interlocutress***; but the case was not made clearer by her presently exclaiming: "I knew you would, from the moment you should be really in love with her! I knew it would be the test -- what do I mean? -- the proof."

"Are there such strange **bewilderments** attached to that high state?" I asked, smiling.

"You perceive there are. You see him, you see him!" Mrs Marden announced, with tremendous ***exaltation***. "You'll see him again."

"I've no objection; but I shall take more interest in him if you'll kindly tell me who he is."

She hesitated, looking down a moment; then she said, raising her eyes: "I'll tell you if you'll tell me first what you said to her on the way to church."

"Has she told you I said anything?"

"Do I need that?" smiled Mrs Marden.

"Oh yes, I remember -- your intuitions! But I'm sorry to see they're at fault this time; because I really said nothing to your daughter that was the least out of the way."

"Are you very sure?"

"On my honour, Mrs Marden."

"Then you consider that you're not in love with her?"

"That's another affair!" I laughed.

"You are -- you ! You wouldn't have seen him if you hadn't been."

"Who the deuce he, then, madam?" I inquired with some ***irritation***.

Panted - *To breathe hard and quickly*
Bewilderments - *To confuse utterly*
Exaltation - *A feeling of intese well-being*
Irritation - *Annoy*

She would still only answer me with another question. "Didn't you at least to say something to her -- didn't you come very near it?"

The question was much to the point; it justified the famous *intuitions*. "Very near it -- it was the turn of a hair. I don't know what kept me quiet."

"That was quite enough," said Mrs Marden. "It isn't what you say that determines it; it's what you feel. what he goes by."

I was annoyed, at last, by her reiterated reference to an identity yet to be established, and I clasped my hands with an air of *supplication* which covered much real impatience, a sharper curiosity and even the first short throbs of a certain sacred dread. "I entreat you to tell me whom you're talking about."

She threw up her arms, looking away from me, as if to shake off both reserve and responsibility. "Sir Edmund Orme."

"And who is Sir Edmund Orme?"

At the moment I spoke she gave a start. "Hush, here they come." Then as, following the direction of her eyes, I saw Charlotte Marden on the terrace, at the window, she added, with an intensity of warning: "Don't notice him -- !"

Charlotte, who had had her hands beside her eyes, peering into the room and smiling, made a sign that she was to be admitted, on which I went and opened the long window. Her mother turned away, and the girl came in with a laughing challenge: "What plot, in the world are you two hatching here?" Some plan -- I forget what -- was in prospect for the afternoon, as to which Mrs Marden's participation or consent was *solicited* -- adhesion was taken for granted -- and she had been half over the place in her quest. I was flurried, because I saw that Mrs Marden was *flurried* (when she turned round to meet her daughter she covered it by a kind of *extravagance*, throwing herself on the girl's neck and embracing her), and to pass it off I said, fancifully, to Charlotte:

"I've been asking your mother for your hand."

"Oh, indeed, and has she given it?" Miss Marden answered, gayly.

"She was just going to when you appeared there."

"Well, it's only for a moment -- I'll leave you free."

"Do you like him, Charlotte?" Mrs Marden asked, with a *candour* I *scarcely* expected.

Intuitions - *Instinctive*
Supplication - *A humble entreaty*
Solicited - *Earnest request*
Flurried - *Marked by confusion or agitation*
Extravagance - *Lavishness*
Candour - *Frankness*
Scarcely - *Hardly*

"It's difficult to say it him isn't it?" the girl replied, entering into the humour of the thing, but looking at me as if she didn't like me.

She would have had to say it before another person as well, for at that moment there stepped into the room from the terrace (the window had been left open), a gentleman who had come into sight, at least into mine, only within the instant. Mrs Marden had said "Here come," but he appeared to have followed her daughter at a certain distance. I immediately recognised him as the ***personage*** who had sat beside us in church. This time I saw him better, saw that his face and his whole air were strange. I speak of him as a personage, because one felt, ***indescribably***, as if a ***reigning*** prince had come into the room. He held himself with a kind of habitual majesty, as if he were different from us. Yet he looked fixedly and gravely at me, till I wondered what he expected of me. Did he consider that I should bend my knee or kiss his hand? He turned his eyes in the same way on Mrs Marden, but she knew what to do. After the first ***agitation*** produced by his approach she took no notice of him whatever; it made me remember her passionate adjuration to me. I had to achieve a great effort to imitate her, for though I knew nothing about him but that he was Sir Edmund Orme I felt his presence as a strong ***appeal***, almost as an ***oppression***. He stood there without speaking -- young, pale, handsome, clean-shaven, decorous, with extraordinary light blue eyes and something old-fashioned, like a portrait of years ago, in his head, his manner of wearing his hair. He was in complete mourning (one immediately felt that he was very well dressed), and he carried his hat in his hand. He looked again strangely hard at me, harder than any one in the world had ever looked before; and I remember feeling rather cold and wishing he would say something. No silence had ever seemed to me so soundless. All this was of course an impression intensely rapid; but that it had consumed some instants was proved to me suddenly by the aspect of Charlotte Marden, who stared from her mother to me and back again (he never looked at her, and she had no appearance of looking at him), and then broke out with: "What on earth is the matter with you? You've such odd faces!" I felt the colour come back to mine, and when she went on in the same tone: "One would think you had seen a ghost!" I was conscious that I had turned very red. Sir Edmund Orme never ***blushed***, and I could see that

Personage - *A person of distinction*
Reigning - *Ruling*
Indescribably - *Indefinable*
Oppression - *Tyranny*
Agitation - *Disturbance*
Blushed - *Embarrassed*

he had no capacity for *embarrassment*. One had met people of that sort, but never any one with such a grand *indifference*.

"Don't be impertinent; and go and tell them all that I'll join them," said Mrs Marden with much *dignity*, but with a *quaver* in her voice.

"And will you come --?" the girl asked, turning away. I made no answer, taking the question, somehow, as meant for her companion. But he was more silent than I, and when she reached the door (she was going out that way), she stopped, with her hand on the knob, and looked at me, repeating it. I assented, springing forward to open the door for her, and as she passed out she exclaimed to me *mockingly*: "You haven't got your wits about you -- you sha'n't have my hand!"

I closed the door and turned round to find that Sir Edmund Orme had during the moment my back was presented to him retired by the window. Mrs Marden stood there and we looked at each other long. It had only then -- as the girl *flitted* away -- come home to me that her daughter was unconscious of what had happened. It was, oddly enough, that gave me a sudden, sharp shake, and not my own perception of our visitor, which appeared perfectly natural. It made the fact vivid to me that she had been equally unaware of him in church, and the two facts together -- now that they were over -- set my heart more sensibly beating. I wiped my forehead, and Mrs Marden broke out with a low *distressful* wail: "Now you know my life -- now you know my life!"

"In God's name who is he -- is he?"

"He's a man I wronged."

"How did you wrong him?"

"Oh, awfully -- years ago."

"Years ago? Why, he's very young."

"Young -- young?" cried Mrs Marden. "He was born before was!"

"Then why does he look so?"

She came nearer to me, she laid her hand on my arm, and there was something in her face that made me *shrink* a little. "Don't you understand -- don't you?" she murmured, reproachfully.

"I feel very queer!" I laughed; and I was conscious that my laugh *betrayed* it.

Indifference - *Unconcerned*
Quaver - *Tremble*
Dignity - *Honour*
Mockingly - *To cause jokingly*
Distressful - *Mentally pain*
Shrink - *Contract, reduce*

"He's dead!" said Mrs Marden, from her white face.

"Dead?" I panted. "Then that gentleman was-?" I couldn't even say the word.

"Call him what you like -- there are twenty *vulgar* names. He's a perfect presence."

"He's a *splendid* presence!" I cried. "The place is haunted -- !" I *exulted* in the word as if it *represented* the *fulfilment* of my dearest dream.

"It isn't the place -- more's the pity! That has nothing to do with it!"

"Then it's you, dear lady?" I said, as if this were still better.

"No, nor me either -- I wish it were!"

"Perhaps it's me," I suggested with a sickly smile.

"It's nobody but my child -- my innocent, *innocent* child!" And with this Mrs Marden broke down -- she dropped into a chair and burst into tears. I *stammered* some question -- I pressed on her some bewildered appeal, but she waved me off, unexpectedly and passionately. I persisted -- couldn't I help her, couldn't I *intervene*? "You intervened," she *sobbed*; "you're it, you're it."

"I'm very glad to be in anything so curious," I boldly declared.

"Glad or not, you can't get out of it."

"I don't want to get out of it -- it's too interesting."

"I'm glad you like it. Go away."

"But I want to know more about it."

"You'll see all you want -- go away!"

"But I want to understand what I see."

"How can you -- when I don't understand myself?"

"We'll do so together -- we'll make it out."

At this she got up, doing what she could to obliterate her tears. "Yes, it will be better together -- that's why I've liked you."

"Oh, we'll see it through!" I declared.

"Then you must control yourself better."

"I will, I will -- with practice."

"You'll get used to it," said Mrs Marden, in a tone I never forgot. "But go and join them -- I'll come in a moment."

Vulgar - *Obscene, indecent*
Fulfilment - *Achievement*
Innocent - *Sinless faultless*
Stammered - *To speak with involuntary breaks and pauses*
Intervene - *To interfere*

I passed out to the terrace and I felt that I had a part to play. So far from *dreading* another encounter with the 'perfect presence', as Mrs Marden called it, I was filled with an excitement that was positively joyous. I desired a renewal of the sensation -- I opened myself wide to the *impression*; I went round the house as quickly as if I expected to overtake Sir Edmund Orme. I didn't overtake him just then, but the day was not to close without my recognising that, as Mrs Marden had said, I should see all I wanted of him.

We took, or most of us took, the collective sociable walk which, in the English country-house, is the consecrated pastime on Sunday afternoons. We were restricted to such a regulated ramble as the ladies were good for; the afternoons, moreover, were short, and by five o'clock we were restored to the fireside in the hall, with a sense, on my part at least, that we might have done a little more for our tea. Mrs Marden had said she would join us, but she had not appeared; her daughter, who had seen her again before we went out, only explained that she was tired. She remained invisible all the afternoon, but this was a detail to which I gave as little heed as I had given to the circumstance of my not having Miss Marden to myself during all our walk. I was too much taken up with another emotion to care; I felt beneath my feet the threshold of the strange door, in my life, which had suddenly been thrown open and out of which unspeakable vibrations played up through me like a *fountain*. I had heard all my days of apparitions, but it was a different thing to have seen one and to know that I should in all *probability* see it familiarly, as it were, again. I was on the look-out for it, as a pilot for the flash of a revolving light, and I was ready to generalise on the *sinister* subject, to declare that ghosts were much less alarming and much more amusing than was commonly supposed. There is no doubt that I was extremely nervous. I couldn't get over the distinction *conferred* upon me -- the exception (in the way of mystic enlargement of vision), made in my favour. At the same time I think I did justice to Mrs Marden's absence; it was a *commentary* on what she had said to me -- "Now you know my life." She had probably been seeing Sir Edmund Orme for years, and, not having my firm fibre, she had broken down under him. Her nerve was gone, though she had also been able to attest that, in a degree, one got used to him. She had got used to breaking down.

Dreading - *Fearing*
Impression - *Impact*
Fountain - *A spring, or source of water*
Sinister - *Bad, evil, wicked*
Conferred - *Granted, bestowed*
Commentary - *A series of comments*

Afternoon tea, when the dusk fell early, was a friendly hour at Tranton; the firelight played into the wide, white last-century hall; sympathies almost confessed themselves, lingering together, before dressing, on deep sofas, in muddy boots, for last words, after walks; and even solitary absorption in the third volume of a novel that was wanted by some one else seemed a form of *geniality*. I watched my moment and went over to Charlotte Marden when I saw she was about to withdraw. The ladies had left the place one by one, and after I had *addressed* myself particularly to Miss Marden the three men who were near her gradually dispersed. We had a little vague talk -- she appeared *preoccupied*, and heaven knows *I* was -- after which she said she must go: she should be late for dinner. I proved to her by book that she had plenty of time, and she objected that she must at any rate go up to see her mother: she was afraid she was unwell.

"On the *contrary*, she's better than she has been for a long time -- I'll *guarantee* that," I said. "She has found out that she can have confidence in me, and that has done her good." Miss Marden had dropped into her chair again. I was standing before her, and she looked up at me without a smile -- with a dim distress in her beautiful eyes; not exactly as if I were hurting her, but as if she were no longer disposed to treat as a joke what had passed (whatever it was, it was at the same time difficult to be serious about it), between her mother and myself. But I could answer her inquiry in all kindness and candour, for I was really conscious that the poor lady had put off a part of her burden on me and was *proportionately* relieved and eased. "I'm sure she has slept all the afternoon as she hasn't slept for years," I went on. "You have only to ask her."

Charlotte got up again. "You make yourself out very useful."

"You've a good quarter of an hour," I said. "Haven't I a right to talk to you a little this way, alone, when your mother has given me your hand?"

"And is it *your* mother who has given me yours? I'm much *obliged* to her, but I don't want it. I think our hands are not our mothers' -- they happen to be our own!" laughed the girl.

"Sit down, sit down and let me tell you!" *I pleaded.*

I still stood before her, urgently, to see if she wouldn't oblige me. She hesitated a moment, looking vaguely this way

Geniality - *Friendly, cordially*
Preoccupied - *Very busy*
Contrary - *Opposite*
Guarantee - *Assurance*
Proportionately - *Balanced*
Obliged - *To bind morally*
Pleaded - *Requested*

and that, as if under a ***compulsion*** that was slightly painful. The empty hall was quiet -- we heard the loud ticking of the great clock. Then she slowly sank down and I drew a chair close to her. This made me face round to the fire again, and with the movement I perceived, disconcertedly, that we were not alone. The next instant, more strangely than I can say, my ***discomposure***, instead of increasing, dropped, for the person before the fire was Sir Edmund Orme. He stood there as I had seen him in the Indian room, looking at me with the expressionless attention which borrowed its sternness from his sombre distinction. I knew so much more about him now that I had to check a movement of ***recognition***, an acknowledgment of his presence. When once I was aware of it, and that it lasted, the sense that we had company, Charlotte and I, quitted me; it was impressed on me on the contrary that I was more intensely alone with Miss Marden. She evidently saw nothing to look at, and I made a tremendous and very nearly successful effort to ***conceal*** from her that my own situation was different. I say 'very nearly', because she watched me an instant -- while my words were arrested -- in a way that made me fear she was going to say again, as she had said in the Indian room: 'What on earth is the matter with you?'

What the matter with me was I quickly told her, for the full knowledge of it rolled over me with the touching spectacle of her unconsciousness. It was touching that she became, in the presence of this extraordinary portent. What was portended, danger or sorrow, bliss or bane, was a minor question; all I saw, as she sat there, was that, innocent and charming, she was close to a horror, as she might have thought it, that happened to be veiled from her but that might at any moment be disclosed. I didn't mind it now, as I found, but nothing was more possible than she should, and if it wasn't curious and interesting it might easily be very dreadful. If I didn't mind it for myself, as I afterwards saw, this was largely because I was so taken up with the idea of protecting *her*. My heart beat high with this idea, on the spot; I determined to do everything I could to keep her sense ***sealed***. What I could do might have been very ***obscure*** to me if I had not, in all this, become more aware than of anything else that I loved her. The way to save her was to love her, and the way to love her was to tell her, now and here, that I did so. Sir Edmund Orme didn't prevent me, especially as after a moment he turned his back to us and stood looking

Compulsion - *Constraint*
Discomposure - *To disturb*
Recognition - *Acceptance*
Conceal - *Hide*
Sealed - *Closed*
Obscure - *Not clear, vague*

discreetly at the fire. At the end of another moment he leaned his head on his arm, against the chimneypiece, with an air of gradual dejection, like a spirit still more weary than **discreet**. Charlotte Marden was startled by what I said to her, and she jumped up to escape it; but she took no offence -- my tenderness was too real. She only moved about the room with a deprecating murmur, and I was so busy following up any little advantage that I might have obtained that I didn't notice in what manner Sir Edmund Orme disappeared. I only observed presently that he had gone. This made no difference -- he had been so small a **hindrance**; I only remember being struck, suddenly, with something inexorable in the slow, sweet, sad headshake that Miss Marden gave me.

"I don't ask for an answer now," I said; "I only want you to be sure -- to know how much depends on it."

"Oh, I don't want to give it to you, now or ever!" she replied. "I hate the subject, please -- I wish one could be let alone." And then, as if I might have found something harsh in this *irrepressible*, artless cry of beauty beset, she added quickly, vaguely, kindly, as she left the room: "Thank you, thank you -- thank you so much!"

At dinner I could be generous enough to be glad, for her, that I was placed on the same side of the table with her, where she couldn't see me. Her mother was nearly opposite to me, and just after we had sat down Mrs Marden gave me one long, deep look, in which all our strange *communion* was expressed. It meant of course 'She has told me,' but it meant other things beside. At any rate I know what my answering look to her *conveyed*: 'I've seen him again -- I've seen him again!' This didn't prevent Mrs Marden from treating her neighbours with her usual scrupulous blandness. After dinner, when, in the drawing-room, the men joined the ladies and I went straight up to her to tell her how I wished we could have some private conversation, she said immediately, in a low tone, looking down at her fan while she opened and shut it:

"He's here -- he's here."

"Here?" I looked round the room, but I was disappointed.

"Look where *she* is," said Mrs Marden, with just the faintest *asperity*. Charlotte was in fact not in the main saloon, but in an apartment into which it opened and which was known as the morning-room. I took a few steps and saw her, through a

Dejection - *Depression, melancholy*
Hindrance - *Obstacle*
Irrepressible - *Uncontrollable*
Asperity - *Bitterness*

doorway, **upright** in the middle of the room, talking with three gentlemen whose backs were practically turned to me. For a moment my quest seemed vain; then I recognised that one of the gentlemen -- the middle one -- was Sir Edmund Orme. This time it *was* surprising that the others didn't see him. Charlotte seemed to be looking straight at him, addressing her conversation to him. She saw me after an instant, however, and immediately turned her eyes away. I went back to her mother with an annoyed sense that the girl would think I was watching *her*, which would be **unjust**. Mrs Marden had found a small sofa -- a little apart -- and I sat down beside her. There were some questions I had so wanted to go into that I wished we were once more in the Indian room. I presently gathered, however, that our *privacy* was all-sufficient. We communicated so closely and completely now, and with such silent *reciprocities*, that it would in every circumstance be adequate.

"Oh, yes, he's there," I said; "and at about a quarter-past seven he was in the hall."

"I knew it at the time, and I was so glad!"

"So glad?"

"That it was your affair, this time, and not mine. It's a rest for me."

"Did you sleep all the afternoon?" I asked.

"As I haven't done for months. But how did you know that?"

"As *you* knew, I take it, that Sir Edmund was in the hall. We shall **evidently** each of us know things now -- where the other is concerned."

"Where *he* is concerned," Mrs Marden amended. "It's a blessing, the way you take it," she added, with a long, mild sigh.

"I take it as a man who's in love with your daughter."

"Of course -- of course." Intense as I now felt my desire for the girl to be, I couldn't help laughing a little at the tone of these words; and it led my *companion* immediately to say: "Otherwise you wouldn't have seen him."

"But every one doesn't see him who's in love with her, or there would be **dozens**."

"They're not in love with her as you are."

"I can, of course, only speak for myself; and I found a moment, before dinner, to do so."

Upright - *Adequate enough*
Unjust - *Unfair*
Reciprocities - *A mutual exchange of ideas*
Evidently - *Clearly*

"She told me immediately."

"And have I any hope -- any chance?"

"That's what *I* long for, what I pray for."

"Ah, how can I thank you enough?" I murmured.

"I believe it will all pass -- if she loves you," Mrs Marden continued.

"It will all pass?"

"We shall never see him again."

"Oh, if she loves me I don't care how often I see him!"

"Ah, you take it better than I could," said my companion. "You have the happiness not to know -- not to understand."

"I don't indeed. What on earth does he want?"

"He wants to make me suffer." She turned her wan face upon me with this, and I saw now for the first time, fully, how perfectly, if this had been Sir Edmund Orme's purpose, he had **succeeded**. "For what I did to him," Mrs Marden explained.

"And what did you do to him?"

She looked at me a moment. "I killed him." As I had seen him fifty yards away only five minutes before the words gave me a start. "Yes, I make you jump; be careful. He's there still, but he killed himself. I broke his heart -- he thought me ***awfully*** bad. We were to have been married, but I broke it off -- just at the last. I saw some one I liked better; I had no reason but that. It wasn't for interest, or money, or position, or anything of that sort. All *those* things were his. It was simply that I fell in love with Captain Marden. When I saw him I felt that I couldn't marry any one else. I wasn't in love with Edmund Orme -- my mother, my elder sister had brought it about. But he did love me. I told him I didn't care -- that I couldn't, that I *wouldn't*. I threw him over, and he took something, some abominable drug or draught that proved ***fatal***. It was dreadful, it was horrible, he was found that way -- he died in agony. I married Captain Marden, but not for five years. I was happy, perfectly happy; time ***obliterates***. But when my husband died I began to see him."

I had listened ***intently***, but I wondered. "To see your husband?"

"Never, never *that* way, thank God! To see *him*, with Chartie -- always with Chartie. The first time it nearly killed me -- about seven years ago, when she first came out. Never

Succeeded
-*Flourished attain a goal*
Awfully - *Horribly*
Fatal - *Deadly, causing death*
Obliterates - *To remove or destory completely*
Intently - *Intensely*

when I'm by myself -- only with her. Sometimes not for months, then every day for a week. I've tried everything to break the *spell* -- doctors and *regimes* and climates; I've prayed to God on my knees. That day at Brighton, on the Parade with you, when you thought I was ill, that was the first for an age. And then, in the evening, when I knocked my tea over you, and the day you were at the door with Charlotte and I saw you from the window -- each time he was there."

"I see, I see." I was more thrilled than I could say. "It's an apparition like another."

"Like another? Have you ever seen another?"

"No, I mean the sort of thing one has heard of. It's tremendously interesting to *encounter* a case."

"Do you call me a 'case'?" Mrs Marden asked, with exquisite resentment.

"I mean myself."

"Oh, you're the right one!" she exclaimed. "I was right when I trusted you."

"I'm devoutly grateful you did; but what made you do it?"

"I had thought the whole thing out -- I had had time to in those dreadful years, while he was punishing me in my daughter."

"Hardly that," I objected, "if she never knew."

"That has been my terror, that she *will*, from one occasion to another. I've an unspeakable dread of the effect on her."

"She sha'n't, she sha'n't!" I declared, so loud that several people looked round. Mrs Marden made me get up, and I had no more talk with her that evening. The next day I told her I must take my departure from Tranton -- it was neither comfortable nor considerate to remain as a *rejected* suitor. She was disconcerted, but she accepted my reasons, only saying to me out of her *mournful* eyes: 'You'll leave me alone then with my burden?' It was of course understood between us that for many weeks to come there would be no discretion in 'worrying poor Charlotte': such were the terms in which, with odd feminine and maternal *inconsistency*, she *alluded* to an attitude on my part that she favoured. I was prepared to be heroically considerate, but it seemed to me that even this delicacy permitted me to say a word to Miss Marden before I went. I begged her, after breakfast, to take a turn with me on the terrace, and as she

Regimes - *Rule, power*
Encounter - *To meet with*
Mournful - *Sorrowful*
Inconsistency - *Incompatibility*
Alluded - *To refer casually*

hesitated, looking at me *distantly*, I informed her that it was only to ask her a question and to say good-bye -- I was leaving Tranton for *her*.

She came out with me, and we passed slowly round the house three or four times. Nothing is finer than this great *airy* platform, from which every look is a sweep of the country, with the sea on the furthest edge. It might have been that as we passed the windows we were *conspicuous* to our friends in the house, who would divine, sarcastically, why I was so significantly *bolting*. But I didn't care; I only wondered whether they wouldn't really this time make out Sir Edmund Orme, who joined us on one of our turns and strolled slowly on the other side of my companion. Of what transcendent essence he was composed I knew not; I have no theory about him (leaving that to others), any more than I have one about such or such another of my fellow-mortals whom I have elbowed in life. He was as positive, as individual, as ultimate a fact as any of these. Above all he was as respectable, as sensitive a fact; so that I should no more have thought of taking a *liberty*, of practicing an experiment with him, of touching him, for instance, or speaking to him, since he set the example of silence, than I should have thought of *committing* any other social grossness. He had always, as I saw more fully later, the perfect propriety of his position -- had always the appearance of being dressed and, in attitude and aspect, of *comporting* himself, as the occasion demanded. He looked strange, incontestably, but somehow he always looked *right*. I very soon came to attach an idea of beauty to his *unmentionable* presence, the beauty of an old story of love and pain. What I ended by feeling was that he was on my side, that he was watching over my interest, that he was looking to it that my heart shouldn't be broken. Oh, he had taken it seriously, his own catastrophe -- he had certainly proved that in his day. If poor Mrs Marden, as she told me, had thought it out, I also subjected the case to the finest analysis of which my intellect was capable. It was a case of retributive justice. The mother was to pay, in suffering, for the suffering she had *inflicted*, and as the *disposition* to jilt a lover might have been *transmitted* to the daughter, the daughter was to be watched, so that *she* might be made to suffer should she do an equal wrong. She might reproduce her mother in character as *vividly* as she did in face. On the day she should transgress, in other

Conspicuous - *Easily seen or noticed*
Disposition - *Find settlement of a matter*
Inflicted - *Imposed*
Vividly - *Cleared*

words, her eyes would be opened suddenly and unpitiedly to the 'perfect presence', which she would have to work as she could into her conception of a young lady's universe. I had no great fear for her, because I didn't believe she was, in any cruel degree, a *coquette*. We should have a good deal of ground to get over before I, at least, should be in a position to be sacrificed by her. She couldn't throw me over before she had made a little more of me.

The question I asked her on the terrace that morning was whether I might continue, during the winter, to come to Mrs Marden's house. I promised not to come too often and not to speak to her for three months of the question I had raised the day before. She replied that I might do as I liked, and on this we parted.

I carried out the vow I had made her; I held my tongue for my three months. Unexpectedly to myself there were moments of this time when she struck me as capable of playing with a man. I wanted so to make her like me that I became subtle and *ingenious*, wonderfully alert, patiently *diplomatic*. Sometimes I thought I had earned my reward, brought her to the point of saying: 'Well, well, you're the best of them all -- you may speak to me now.' Then there was a greater *blankness* than ever in her beauty, and on certain days a mocking light in her eyes, of which the meaning seemed to be: 'If you don't take care, I *will* accept you, to have done with you the more effectually.' Mrs Marden was a great help to me simply by believing in me, and I valued her faith all the more that it continued even though there was a sudden *intermission* of the miracle that had been wrought for me. After our visit to Tranton Sir Edmund Orme gave us a holiday, and I confess it was at first a disappointment to me. I felt less *designated*, less connected with Charlotte. "Oh, don't cry till you're out of the wood," her mother said; "he has let me off sometimes for six months. He'll break out again when you least expect it -- he knows what he's about." For her these weeks were happy, and she was wise enough not to talk about me to the girl. She was so good as to assure me that I was taking the right way, that I looked as if I felt secure and that in the long run women give way to that. She had known them do it even when the man was a fool for looking so -- or was a fool on any terms. For herself she felt it to be a good time, a sort of St Martin's summer of the soul. She was better than she had

Coquette - *Flirted*
Ingenious - *Gifted*
Diplomatic - *Tactful*
Intermission - *Interval*
Designated - *Indicated, nominated*

Greatest Ghost Stories

been for years, and she had me to thank for it. The sense of visitation was light upon her -- she wasn't in *anguish* every time she looked around. Charlotte contradicted me very often, but she *contradicted* herself still more. That winter was a wonder of *mildness*, and we often sat out in the sun. I walked up and down with Charlotte, and Mrs Marden, sometimes on a bench, sometimes in a bath-chair, waited for us and smiled at us as we passed. I always looked out for a sign in her face -- 'He's with you, he's with you' (she would see him before I should), but nothing came; the season had brought us also a sort of spiritual softness. Toward the end of April the air was so like June that, meeting my two friends one night at some Brighton *sociability* -- an evening party with *amateur* music -- I drew Miss Marden unresistingly out upon a balcony to which a window in one of the rooms stood open. The night was close and thick, the stars were dim, and below us, under the cliff, we heard the regular rumble of the sea. We listened to it a little and we heard mixed with it, from within the house, the sound of a violin accompanied by a piano -- a performance which had been our pretext for passing out.

"Do you like me a little better?" I asked, abruptly, after a minute. "Could you listen to me again?" I had no sooner spoken than she laid her hand quickly, with a certain force, on my arm. "Hush! -- isn't there some one there?" She was looking into the gloom of the far end of the balcony. This balcony ran the whole width of the house, a width very great in the best of the old houses at Brighton. We were lighted a little by the open window behind us, but the other windows, curtained within, left the darkness *undiminished*, so that I made out but dimly the figure of a gentleman standing there and looking at us. He was in evening dress, like a guest -- I saw the vague shine of his white shirt and the pale oval of his face -- and he might perfectly have been a guest who had stepped out in advance of us to take the air. Miss Marden took him for one at first -- then evidently, even in a few seconds, she saw that the intensity of his *gaze* was *unconventional*. What else she saw I couldn't determine; I was too taken up with my own impression to do more than feel the quick contact of her uneasiness. My own impression was in fact the strongest of sensations, a sensation of horror; for what could the thing mean but that the girl at last *saw*? I heard her give a sudden, *gasping* "Ah!" and move quickly into the house. It was only

Contradicted
- *Anguish tormented, for turned*
Amateur - *Novice*
Undiminished - *Not reduced*
Gaze - *To look steadily and intently*
Gasping - *Sudden short in take of breath*

afterwards that I knew that I myself had had a totally new emotion -- my horror passing into anger, and my anger into a stride along the balcony with a *gesture* of *reprobation*. The case was *simplified* to the vision of a frightened girl whom I loved. I advanced to *vindicate* her security, but I found nothing there to meet me. It was either all a mistake or Sir Edmund Orme had *vanished*.

I followed Miss Marden immediately, but there were symptoms of confusion in the drawing-room when I passed in. A lady had fainted, the music had stopped; there was a *shuffling* of chairs and a pressing forward. The lady was not Charlotte, as I feared, but Mrs Marden, who had suddenly been taken ill. I remember the relief with which I learned this, for to see Charlotte stricken would have been *anguish*, and her mother's condition gave a channel to her agitation. It was of course all a matter for the people of the house and for the ladies, and I could have no share in attending to my friends or in conducting them to their carriage. Mrs Marden revived and insisted on going home, after which I uneasily withdrew.

I called the next morning to ask about her and was informed that she was better, but when I asked if Miss Marden would see me the message sent down was that it was impossible. There was nothing for me to do all day but to roam about with a beating heart. But toward evening I received a line in pencil, brought by hand -- 'Please come; mother wishes you.' Five minutes afterward was at the door again and *ushered* into the drawing-room. Mrs Marden lay upon the sofa, and as soon as I looked at her I saw the shadow of death in her face. But the first thing she said was that she was better, ever so much better; her poor old heart had been behaving queerly again, but now it was quiet. She gave me her hand and I bent over her with my eyes in hers, and in this way I was able to read what she didn't speak -- 'I'm really very ill, but appear to take what I say exactly as I say it.' Charlotte stood there beside her, looking not frightened now, but intensely *grave*, and not meeting my eyes. "She has told me -- she has told me!" her mother went on.

"She has told you?" I *stared* from one of them to the other, wondering if Mrs Marden meant that the girl had spoken to her of the circumstances on the balcony.

Simplified - *Made easy*
Vanished - *Disappeared*
Shuffling - *To inter mix*
Ushered - *To lead or herald*
Grave - *Very serious, solemn*
Stared - *To look or gaze fixedly*

Greatest Ghost Stories

"That you spoke to her again -- that you're admirably faithful."

I felt a thrill of joy at this; it showed me that that memory had been uppermost, and also that Charlotte had wished to say the thing that would soothe her mother most, not the thing that would *alarm* her. Yet I now knew, myself, as well as if Mrs Marden had told me, that she knew and had known at the moment what her daughter had seen. "I spoke -- I spoke, but she gave me no answer," I said.

"She will now, won't you, Chartie? I want it so, I want it!" the poor lady murmured, with *ineffable wistfulness*.

"You're very good to me," Charlotte said to me, seriously and sweetly, looking fixedly on the carpet. There was something different in her, different from all the past. She had recognised something, she felt a coercion. I could see that she was trembling.

"Ah, if you would let me show you *how* good I can be!" I exclaimed, holding out my hands to her. As I uttered the words I was touched with the knowledge that something had happened. A form had constituted itself on the other side of the bed, and the form leaned over Mrs Marden. My whole being went forth into a *mute* prayer that Charlotte shouldn't see it and that I should be able to betray nothing. The impulse to glance toward Mrs Marden was even stronger than the involuntary movement of taking in Sir Edmund Orme; but I could resist even that, and Mrs Marden was perfectly still. Charlotte got up to give me her hand, and with the definite act she saw. She gave, with a *shriek*, one stare of dismay, and another sound, like a wail of one of the lost, fell at the same instant on my ear. But I had already *sprung* toward the girl to cover her, to *veil* her face. She had already thrown herself into my arms. I held her there a moment -- bending over her, given up to her, feeling each of her throbs with my own and not knowing which was which; then, all of a sudden, coldly, I gathered that we were alone. She released herself. The figure beside the sofa had vanished; but Mrs Marden lay in her place with closed eyes, with something in her *stillness* that gave us both another terror. Charlotte expressed it in the cry of "Mother, mother!" with which she flung herself down. I fell on my knees beside her. Mrs Marden had passed away.

Alarm - *Warn*
Ineffable - *Inexpressable*
Wistfulness - *Sadness*
Shriek - *A loud, sharp, shrill cry*
Veil - *Mask*

Was the sound I heard when Chartie shrieked -- the other and still more tragic sound I mean -- the *despairing* cry of the poor lady's death-shock or the articulate sob (it was like a waft from a great tempest), of the *exorcised* and *pacified* spirit? Possibly the latter, for that was, mercifully, the last of Sir Edmund Orme.

Despairing - *Hopeless*
Exorcised - *To seek to expel, to free*
Pacified - *To appease, soothe*

Food For Thought

Mrs. Marden reveals that in her youth she was a 'bad' girl like her daughter, and so she has been punished for it through life. What did she mean by saying so? Do you feel such incidents occur in real life? Support your answer with reasons.

An Understanding

Q. 1. Who is Sir Edmund Orme and why does his ghost appear time and again in the story harassing Mrs. Marden, a widow and her daughter, Charlotte? What relationship does Mrs. Marden share with Sir Edmund Orme?
Ans. _____
_____
_____
_____
_____

Q. 2. Who is the narrator of the story and what relationship does he have with Mr.s Marden and her daughter?
Ans. _____
_____
_____
_____
_____

Q. 3. Why does Charlotte decline the offer of the narrator to marry her and what happens when the narrator proposes her for the second time?
Ans. _____
_____
_____
_____
_____

Q. 4. How does Mrs. Marden die? Why did the ghost of Sir Edmund Orme appear every time the narrator proposed Mrs. Marden's daughter, Charlotte?
Ans. _____
_____
_____
_____
_____

The Phantom Coach
~Amelia Edwards

THe circumstances I am about to relate to you have truth to recommend them. They happened to myself, and my recollection of them is as vivid as if they had taken place only yesterday. Twenty years, however, have gone by since that night. During those twenty years I have told the story to but one other person. I tell it now with a reluctance which I find it difficult to overcome. All I entreat, meanwhile, is that you will abstain from forcing your own *conclusions* upon me. I want nothing explained away. I desire no arguments. My mind on this subject is quite made up, and, having the testimony of my own senses to rely upon, I prefer to abide by it.

Well! It was just twenty years ago, and within a day or two of the end of the *grouse* season. I had been out all day with my gun, and had had no sport to speak of. The wind was due east; the month, December; the place, a bleak wide moor in the far north of England. And I had lost my way. It was not a pleasant place in which to lose one's way, with the first feathery flakes of a coming snowstorm just *fluttering* down upon the heather, and the leaden evening closing in all around. I shaded my eyes with my hand, and staled anxiously into the gathering darkness, where the purple *moorland* melted into a range of low hills, some ten or twelve miles distant. Not the faintest smoke-wreath, not the tiniest cultivated patch, or fence, or sheep-track, met my eyes in any direction. There was nothing for it but to walk on, and take my chance of finding what shelter I could, by the way. So I shouldered my gun again, and pushed *wearily* forward; for I had been on foot since an hour after daybreak, and had eaten nothing since breakfast.

Meanwhile, the snow began to come down with ominous *steadiness*, and the wind fell. After this, the cold became more intense, and the night came rapidly up. As for me, my prospects darkened with the darkening sky, and my heart grew heavy as I thought how my young wife was already watching for me through the window of our little *inn parlour*, and thought of all the suffering in store for her throughout this weary night. We had been married four months, and, having spent our autumn in the Highlands, were now lodging in a remote little village situated just on the *verge* of the great English

Conclusions - *Results*
Grouse - *A complaint*
Fluttering - *Vibratting*
Wearily - *Tiredly*
Inn - *Small hotel*
Verge - *Edge*

moorlands. We were very much in love, and, of course, very happy. This morning, when we parted, she had implored me to return before *dusk*, and I had promised her that I would. What would I not have given to have kept my word!

Even now, *weary* as I was, I felt that with a *supper*, an hour's rest, and a guide, I might still get back to her before midnight, if only guide and shelter could be found.

And all this time, the snow fell and the night thickened. I stopped and shouted every now and then, but my shouts seemed only to make the silence deeper. Then a vague sense of uneasiness came upon me, and I began to remember stories of travellers who had walked on and on in the falling snow until, wearied out, they were fain to lie down and sleep their lives away. Would it be possible, I asked myself, to keep on thus through all the long dark night? Would there not come a time when my limbs must fail, and my resolution give way? When I, too, must sleep the sleep of death. Death! I shuddered. How hard to die just now, when life lay all so bright before me! How hard for my darling, whose whole loving heart but that thought was not to be borne! To *banish* it, I shouted again, louder and longer, and then listened eagerly. Was my shout answered, or did I only fancy that I heard a far-off cry? I *halloed* again, and again the echo followed. Then a wavering speck of light came suddenly out of the dark, shifting, disappearing, growing *momentarily* nearer and brighter. Running towards it at full speed, I found myself, to my great joy, face to face with an old man and a *lantern*.

"Thank God!" was the *exclamation* that burst involuntarily from my lips.

Blinking and frowning, he lifted his lantern and peered into my face.

"What for?" growled he, *sulkily*.

"Well -- for you. I began to fear I should be lost in the snow."

"Eh, then, folks do get cast away *hereabouts* fra' time to time, an' what's to hinder you from bein' cast away likewise, if the Lord's so minded?"

"If the Lord is so minded that you and I shall be lost together, friend, we must submit," I replied; "but I don't mean to be lost without you. How far am I now from Dwolding?"

"A gude twenty mile, more or less."

"And the nearest village?"

Moorlands - *Tracts of open countryside*
Dusk - *Twilight*
Banshi - *Deport*
Halloed - *Shouted*
Lantern - *Lamp, light*
Sulkily - *Gloomily*

"The nearest village is Wyke, an' that's twelve mile t'other side."

"Where do you live, then?"

"Out **yonder**," said he, with a **vague jerk** of the lantern.

"You're going home, I **presume**?"

"Maybe I am."

"Then I'm going with you."

The old man shook his head, and rubbed his nose **reflectively** with the handle of the lantern.

"It ain't o' no use," growled he. "He 'ont let you in -- not he."

"We'll see about that," I replied, **briskly**. "Who is He?"

"The master."

"Who is the master?"

"That's nowt to you," was the **unceremonious** reply.

"Well, well; you lead the way, and I'll engage that the master shall give me shelter and a supper to-night."

"Eh, you can try him!" muttered my **reluctant** guide; and, still shaking his head, he hobbled, gnome-like, away through the falling snow. A large mass **loomed** up presently out of the darkness, and a huge dog rushed out, barking furiously.

"Is this the house?" I asked.

"Ay, it's the house. Down, Bey!" And he fumbled in his pocket for the key.

I drew up close behind him, prepared to lose no chance of entrance, and saw in the little circle of light shed by the lantern that the door was heavily **studded** with iron nails, like the door of a prison. In another minute he had turned the key and I had pushed past him into the house.

Once inside, I looked round with curiosity, and found myself in a great raftered hall, which served, **apparently**, a variety of uses. One end was piled to the roof with corn, like a barn. The other was stored with flour-sacks, agricultural implements, casks, and all kinds of **miscellaneous lumber**; while from the beams overhead hung rows of hams, flitches, and bunches of dried herbs for winter use. In the centre of the floor stood some huge object **gauntly** dressed in a **dingy** wrapping-cloth, and reaching half way to the rafters. Lifting a corner of this cloth, I saw, to my surprise, a **telescope** of very considerable size, mounted on a rude movable platform, with four small wheels. The tube was made of painted wood, bound

Loomed - *To come into view vaguely*
Yonder - *Over these*
Unceremonious - *Discourteously*
Reluctant - *Unwilling*
Studded - *To set shaffy*
Gauntly - *Very thin and bony*

round with bands of metal *rudely* fashioned; the *speculum*, so far as I could estimate its size in the dim light, measured at least fifteen inches in diameter. While I was yet examining the instrument, and asking myself whether it was not the work of some *self-taught* optician, a bell rang sharply.

"That's for you," said my guide, with a *malicious* grin. "Yonder's his room."

He pointed to a low black door at the opposite side of the hall. I crossed over, rapped somewhat loudly, and went in, without waiting for an invitation. A huge, white-haired old man rose from a table covered with books and papers, and confronted me *sternly*.

"Who are you?" said he. "How came you here? What do you want?"

"James Murray, barrister-at-law. On foot across the moor. Meat, drink, and sleep."

He bent his bushy brows into a *portentous frown*.

"Mine is not a house of entertainment," he said, haughtily. "Jacob, how dared you admit this stranger?"

"I didn't admit him," grumbled the old man. "He followed me over the *muir*, and shouldered his way in before me. I'm no match for six foot two."

"And pray, sir, by what right have you forced an entrance into my house?"

"The same by which I should have *clung* to your boat, if I were drowning. The right of self-preservation."

"Self-preservation?"

"There's an inch of snow on the ground already," I replied, briefly; "and it would be deep enough to cover my body before daybreak."

He strode to the window, pulled aside a heavy black curtain, and looked out.

"It is true," he said. "You can stay, if you choose, till morning. Jacob, serve the supper."

With this he waved me to a seat, *resumed* his own, and became at once absorbed in the studies from which I had disturbed him.

I placed my gun in a corner, drew a chair to the *hearth*, and examined my quarters at leisure. Smaller and less *incongruous* in its arrangements than the hall, this room contained,

---

Speculum - *A mirror*
Malicious - *Mischievous*
Sternly - *Firmly*
Portentous - *Momentous*
Frown - *Scowl*
Muir - *Open tracts of the countryside*
Hearth - *The floor of a fireplace*
Incongruous - *Inappropriate*
Resumed - *To begin again*

nevertheless, much to *awaken* my curiosity. The floor was carpetless. The *whitewashed* walls were in parts scrawled over with strange diagrams, and in others covered with shelves crowded with *philosophical* instruments, the uses of many of which were unknown to me. On one side of the fireplace, stood a bookcase filled with dingy folios; on the other, a small organ, *fantastically* decorated with painted carvings of medieval saints and devils. Through the half-opened door of a cupboard at the further end of the room, I saw a long array of geological *specimens*, surgical preparations, crucibles, retorts, and jars of chemicals; while on the mantelshelf beside me, amid a number of small objects, stood a model of the solar system, a small galvanic battery, and a microscope. Every chair had its burden. Every corner was heaped high with books. The very floor was *littered* over with maps, casts, papers, *tracings*, and learned lumber of all *conceivable* kinds.

I stared about me with an amazement increased by every fresh object upon which my eyes chanced to rest. So strange a room I had never seen; yet seemed it stranger still, to find such a room in a lone farmhouse amid those wild and solitary moors! Over and over again, I looked from my host to his surroundings, and from his surroundings back to my host, asking myself who and what he could be? His head was singularly fine; but it was more the head of a poet than of a philosopher. Broad in the temples, prominent over the eyes, and clothed with a rough *profusion* of perfectly white hair, it had all the ideality and much of the ruggedness that characterises the head of Louis von Beethoven. There were the same deep lines about the mouth, and the same stern furrows in the brow. There was the same concentration of expression. While I was yet observing him, the door opened, and Jacob brought in the supper. His master then closed his book, rose, and with more courtesy of manner than he had yet shown, invited me to the table.

A dish of ham and eggs, a loaf of brown bread, and a bottle of admirable *sherry*, were placed before me.

"I have but the homeliest farmhouse fare to offer you, sir," said my entertainer. "Your appetite, I trust, will make up for the *deficiencies* of our larder."

I had already fallen upon the viands, and now protested, with the enthusiasm of a starving sportsman, that I had never eaten anything so *delicious*.

Specimens - *Types, patterns*
Littered - *Scattered*
Conceivable - *Capable of being understood*
Profusion - *Abundance*
Sherry - *A fortified, amber coloured wine of spain*

He bowed *stiffly*, and sat down to his own supper, which consisted, *primitively*, of a jug of milk and a basin of *porridge*. We ate in silence, and, when we had done, Jacob removed the tray. I then drew my chair back to the fireside. My host, somewhat to my surprise, did the same, and turning abruptly towards me, said:

"Sir, I have lived here in strict retirement for three-and-twenty years. During that time, I have not seen as many strange faces, and I have not read a single newspaper. You are the first stranger who has crossed my *threshold* for more than four years. Will you favour me with a few words of information respecting that outer world from which I have parted company so long?"

"Pray *interrogate* me," I replied. "I am heartily at your service."

He bent his head in *acknowledgment*; leaned forward, with his elbows resting on his knees and his chin supported in the palms of his hands; stared fixedly into the fire; and proceeded to question me.

His inquiries related chiefly to scientific matters, with the later progress of which, as applied to the practical purposes of life, he was almost wholly unacquainted. No student of science myself, I replied as well as my slight information permitted; but the task was far from easy, and I was much relieved when, passing from interrogation to discussion, he began pouring forth his own conclusions upon the facts which I had been attempting to place before him. He talked, and I listened *spellbound*. He talked till I believe he almost forgot my presence, and only thought aloud. I had never heard anything like it then; I have never heard anything like it since. Familiar with all systems of all philosophies, subtle in analysis, bold in generalisation, he poured forth his thoughts in an uninterrupted stream, and, still leaning forward in the same moody attitude with his eyes fixed upon the fire, wandered from topic to topic, from speculation to *speculation*, like an inspired dreamer. From practical science to mental philosophy; from electricity in the wire to electricity in the nerve; from Watts to Mesmer, from Mesmer to Reichenbach, from Reichenbach to Swedenborg, Spinoza, Condillac, Descartes, Berkeley, Aristotle, Plato, and the Magi and mystics of the East, were *transitions* which, however *bewildering* in their variety and scope, seemed easy and *harmonious* upon his lips

Stiffly - *Rigidly*
Porridge - *A food made of oatmeal*
Threshold - *sill of doorway*
Transitions - *Changes*
Bewildering - *Astonishing*
Harmonious - *Peaceful*

as *sequences* in music. By-and-by -- I forget now by what link of conjecture or illustration -- he passed on to that field which lies beyond the boundary line of even *conjectural* philosophy, and reaches no man knows whither. He spoke of the soul and its aspirations; of the spirit and its powers; of second sight; of prophecy; of those phenomena which, under the names of ghosts, spectres, and *supernatural* appearances, have been denied by the sceptics and attested by the credulous, of all ages.

"The world," he said, "grows hourly more and more sceptical of all that lies beyond its own narrow radius; and our men of science foster the fatal tendency. They condemn as fable all that resists experiment. They reject as false all that cannot be brought to the test of the laboratory or the dissecting-room. Against what superstition have they waged so long and obstinate a war, as against the belief in apparitions? And yet what superstition has maintained its hold upon the minds of men so long and so firmly? Show me any fact in physics, in history, in archæology, which is supported by testimony so wide and so various. Attested by all races of men, in all ages, and in all climates, by the *soberest* sages of antiquity, by the rudest savage of to-day, by the Christian, the Pagan, the Pantheist, the Materialist, this phenomenon is treated as a nursery tale by the philosophers of our century. Circumstantial evidence weighs with them as a feather in the balance. The comparison of causes with effects, however valuable in physical science, is put aside as worthless and *unreliable*. The evidence of competent witnesses, however conclusive in a court of justice, counts for nothing. He who pauses before he pronounces, is condemned as a *trifler*. He who believes, is a dreamer or a fool."

He spoke with bitterness, and, having said thus, relapsed for some minutes into silence. Presently he raised his head from his hands, and added, with an altered voice and manner, "I, sir, paused, investigated, believed, and was not ashamed to state my *convictions* to the world. I, too, was branded as a visionary, held up to *ridicule* by my contemporaries, and hooted from that field of science in which I had laboured with honour during all the best years of my life. These things happened just three-and-twenty years ago. Since then, I have lived as you see me living now, and the world has forgotten me, as I have forgotten the world. You have my history."

"It is a very sad one," I murmured, *scarcely* knowing what to answer.

Conjectural - *Doubtful*
Supernatural - *Miraculous*
Trifler - *Idler*
Convictions- *Belief*
Ridicule - *Mock*

"It is a very common one," he replied. "I have only suffered for the truth, as many a better and wiser man has suffered before me."

He rose, as if *desirous* of ending the conversation, and went over to the window.

"It has ceased snowing," he observed, as he dropped the curtain, and came back to the fireside.

"Ceased!" I exclaimed, starting eagerly to my feet. "Oh, if it were only possible -- but no! it is hopeless. Even if I could find my way across the moor, I could not walk twenty miles to-night."

"Walk twenty miles to-night!" repeated my host. "What are you thinking of?"

"Of my wife," I replied, *impatiently*. "Of my young wife, who does not know that I have lost my way, and who is at this moment breaking her heart with suspense and terror."

"Where is she?"

"At Dwolding, twenty miles away."

"At Dwolding," he *echoed*, thoughtfully. "Yes, the distance, it is true, is twenty miles; but -- are you so very anxious to save the next six or eight hours?"

"So very, very anxious, that I would give ten guineas at this moment for a guide and a horse."

"Your wish can be *gratified* at a less costly rate," said he, smiling. "The night mail from the north, which changes horses at Dwolding, passes within five miles of this spot, and will be due at a certain *crossroad* in about an hour and a quarter. If Jacob were to go with you across the moor, and put you into the old coach-road, you could find your way, I suppose, to where it joins the new one?"

"Easily -- gladly."

He smiled again, rang the bell, gave the old servant his directions, and, taking a bottle of whisky and a wineglass from the cupboard in which he kept his chemicals, said:

"The snow lies deep, and it will be difficult walking to-night on the moor. A glass of *usquebaugh* before you start?"

I would have *declined* the spirit, but he pressed it on me, and I drank it. It went down my throat like liquid flame, and almost took my breath away.

Impatiently - *Uneasily*
Echoed - *A repetittion of sound*
Gratified - *Obliged, greatful*
Crossroad - *A road that crosses anohter road*
Usquebaugh - *The other name of whiskey in*
Declined -

"It is strong," he said; "but it will help to keep out the cold. And now you have no moments to spare. Good night!"

I thanked him for his *hospitality*, and would have shaken hands, but that he had turned away before I could finish my sentence. In another minute I had traversed the hall, Jacob had locked the outer door behind me, and we were out on the wide white moor.

Although the wind had fallen, it was still *bitterly* cold. Not a star *glimmered* in the black *vault* overhead. Not a sound, save the rapid *crunching* of the snow beneath our feet, disturbed the heavy stillness of the night. Jacob, not too well pleased with his mission, *shambled* on before in sullen silence, his lantern in his hand, and his shadow at his feet. I followed, with my gun over my shoulder, as little inclined for conversation as himself. My thoughts were full of my late host. His voice yet rang in my ears. His *eloquence* yet held my imagination captive. I remember to this day, with surprise, how my over-excited brain retained whole sentences and parts of sentences, troops of brilliant images, and *fragments* of splendid reasoning, in the very words in which he had uttered them. Musing thus over what I had heard, and *striving* to recall a lost link here and there, I strode on at the heels of my guide, absorbed and *unobservant*. Presently -- at the end, as it seemed to me, of only a few minutes -- he came to a sudden halt, and said:

"Yon's your road. Keep the stone fence to your right hand, and you can't fail of the way."

"This, then, is the old coach-road?"

"Ay, 'tis the old coach-road."

"And how far do I go, before I reach the cross-roads?"

"Nigh upon three mile."

I pulled out my purse, and he became more *communicative*.

"The road's a fair road enough," said he, "for foot passengers; but 'twas over steep and narrow for the northern traffic. You'll mind where the *parapet's* broken away, close again the sign-post. It's never been mended since the accident."

"What accident?"

"Eh, the night mail pitched right over into the valley below -- a gude fifty feet an' more -- just at the worst bit o' road in the whole county."

"Horrible! Were many lives lost?"

Hospitality -
bitterly -
Glimmered -
Crunching -
Shambled -
Eloquence -
Fragments -
Unobservant -
Communicative -
Communicative -
Parapets -

"All. Four were found dead, and t'other two died next morning."

"How long is it since this happened?"

"Just nine year."

"Near the sign-post, you say? I will bear it in mind. Good night."

"Gude night, sir, and thankee." Jacob *pocketed* his half-crown, made a faint *pretence* of touching his hat, and *trudged* back by the way he had come.

I watched the light of his lantern till it quite disappeared, and then turned to pursue my way alone. This was no longer matter of the slightest difficulty, for, despite the dead darkness overhead, the line of stone fence showed distinctly enough against the pale gleam of the snow. How silent it seemed now, with only my footsteps to listen to; how silent and how solitary!

A strange *disagreeable* sense of loneliness stole over me. I walked faster. I *hummed* a fragment of a tune. I cast up enormous sums in my head, and *accumulated* them at compound interest. I did my best, in short, to forget the *startling speculations* to which I had but just been listening, and, to some extent, I succeeded.

Meanwhile the night air seemed to become colder and colder, and though I walked fast I found it impossible to keep myself warm. My feet were like ice. I lost sensation in my hands, and grasped my gun mechanically. I even breathed with difficulty, as though, instead of *traversing* a quiet north country highway, I were scaling the uppermost heights of some gigantic Alp. This last symptom became presently so *distressing*, that I was forced to stop for a few minutes, and lean against the stone fence.

As I did so, I chanced to look back up the road, and there, to my infinite relief, I saw a distant point of light, like the gleam of an approaching lantern. I at first concluded that Jacob had *retraced* his steps and followed me; but even as the *conjecture* presented itself, a second light flashed into sight -- a light evidently parallel with the first, and approaching at the same rate of motion.

It needed no second thought to show me that these must be the carriage-lamps of some private vehicle, though it seemed

Pocketed - *Stole, filched*
Trudged - *To walk or plod heavily*
Hummed - *To make a low, continuous droning sound*
Startling - *Astonishing*
Speculations - *Assumptions, suppositions*
Traversing - *Crossing*
Conjecture - *Theory, hypothesis*

strange that any private vehicle should take a road professedly disused and dangerous.

There could be no doubt, however, of the fact, for the lamps grew larger and brighter every moment, and I even ***fancied*** I could already see the dark outline of the carriage between them. It was coming up very fast, and quite noiselessly, the snow being nearly a foot deep under the wheels.

And now the body of the vehicle became distinctly visible behind the lamps. It looked strangely lofty. A sudden ***suspicion*** flashed upon me. Was it possible that I had passed the cross-roads in the dark without observing the sign-post, and could this be the very coach which I had come to meet?

No need to ask myself that question a second time, for here it came round the bend of the road, guard and driver, one outside passenger, and four steaming greys, all wrapped in a soft ***haze*** of light, through which the lamps ***blazed*** out, like a pair of ***fiery meteors.***

I jumped forward, waved my hat, and shouted. The mail came down at full speed, and passed me. For a moment I feared that I had not been seen or heard, but it was only for a moment. The coachman pulled up; the guard, muffled to the eyes in capes and comforters, and apparently sound asleep in the rumble, neither answered my ***hail*** nor made the slightest effort to dismount; the outside passenger did not even turn his head.

I opened the door for myself, and looked in. There were but three travellers inside, so I stepped in, shut the door, slipped into the vacant corner, and congratulated myself on my good fortune.

The atmosphere of the coach seemed, if possible, colder than that of the outer air, and was pervaded by a singularly ***damp*** and disagreeable smell. I looked round at my fellow-passengers. They were all three, men, and all silent. They did not seem to be asleep, but each leaned back in his corner of the vehicle, as if absorbed in his own reflections. I ***attempted*** to open a conversation.

"How intensely cold it is to-night," I said, addressing my opposite neighbour.

He lifted his head, looked at me, but made no reply.

"The winter," I added, "seems to have begun in ***earnest***."

Meteros - *Shooting stars*
Suspicion - *Doubt*
Haze - *Obscurity of perception*
Hail - *To cheer, salute*
Damp - *Slightly wet*
Attempted - *To make an effort at*
Earnest - *Sincere*

Although the corner in which he sat was so dim that I could distinguish none of his features very clearly, I saw that his eyes were still turned full upon me. And yet he answered never a word.

At any other time I should have felt, and perhaps expressed, some ***annoyance***, but at the moment I felt too ill to do either. The icy coldness of the night air had struck a chill to my very ***marrow***, and the strange smell inside the coach was affecting me with an ***intolerable nausea***. I shivered from head to foot, and, turning to my left-hand neighbour, asked if he had any objection to an open window?

He neither spoke nor stirred.

I repeated the question somewhat more loudly, but with the same result. Then I lost patience, and let the ***sash*** down. As I did so, the leather strap broke in my hand, and I observed that the glass was covered with a thick coat of mildew, the accumulation, apparently, of years. My attention being thus drawn to the condition of the coach, I examined it more narrowly, and saw by the uncertain light of the outer lamps that it was in the last stage of ***dilapidation***. Every part of it was not only out of repair, but in a condition of decay.

The sashes splintered at a touch. The leather fittings were crusted over with mould, and literally rotting from the woodwork. The floor was almost breaking away beneath my feet. The whole machine, in short, was foul with damp, and had evidently been dragged from some outhouse in which it had been mouldering away for years, to do another day or two of duty on the road.

I turned to the third passenger, whom I had not yet addressed, and hazarded one more remark.

"This coach," I said, "is in a deplorable condition. The regular mail, I suppose, is under repair?"

He moved his head slowly, and looked me in the face, without speaking a word. I shall never forget that look while I live. I turned cold at heart under it. I turn cold at heart even now when I recall it. His eyes glowed with a fiery unnatural lustre. His face was livid as the face of a corpse. His bloodless lips were drawn back as if in the agony of death, and showed the gleaming teeth between.

The words that I was about to utter died upon my lips, and a strange horror -- a dreadful horror -- came upon me.

Marrow - *Fluid inside the bone*
Intolerable - *Unbearable*
Nausea - *Vomiting sensation*
Dilapidation - *Destructive event*
Gloom - *Sad*

My sight had by this time become used to the *gloom* of the coach, and I could see with tolerable distinctness. I turned to my opposite neighbour. He, too, was looking at me, with the same *startling pallor* in his face, and the same stony glitter in his eyes. I passed my hand across my brow. I turned to the passenger on the seat beside my own, and saw -- oh Heaven! how shall I describe what I saw? I saw that he was no living man -- that none of them were living men, like myself!

A pale *phosphorescent* light -- the light of *putrefaction* -- played upon their awful faces; upon their hair, dank with the dews of the grave; upon their clothes, earth-stained and dropping to pieces; upon their hands, which were as the hands of corpses long buried. Only their eyes, their terrible eyes, were living; and those eyes were all turned menacingly upon me!

A shriek of terror, a wild *unintelligible* cry for help and mercy; burst from my lips as I flung myself against the door, and *strove* in *vain* to open it.

In that single instant, brief and vivid as a landscape beheld in the flash of summer lightning, I saw the moon shining down through a rift of stormy cloud -- the ghastly sign-post rearing its warning finger by the wayside -- the broken *parapet* -- the *plunging* horses -- the black gulf below. Then, the coach reeled like a ship at sea. Then, came a mighty crash -- a sense of crushing pain -- and then, darkness.

It seemed as if years had gone by when I awoke one morning from a deep sleep, and found my wife watching by my bedside I will pass over the scene that ensued, and give you, in half a dozen words, the tale she told me with tears of thanksgiving. I had fallen over a precipice, close against the junction of the old coach-road and the new, and had only been saved from certain death by lighting upon a deep *snowdrift* that had accumulated at the foot of the rock beneath. In this snowdrift I was discovered at daybreak, by a couple of shepherds, who carried me to the nearest shelter, and brought a surgeon to my aid.

The surgeon found me in a state of raving *delirium*, with a broken arm and a compound fracture of the skull. The letters in my pocket-book showed my name and address; my wife was *summoned* to nurse me; and, thanks to youth and a fine constitution, I came out of danger at last. The place of my

Pallor- *Unusual or extreme paleness*
Unintelligible - *Not capable*
Vain - *Proud*
Plunging - *Diving*
Delirium - *Mental confusion*
Summoned - *To call upon*

fall, I need scarcely say, was precisely that at which a frightful accident had happened to the north mail nine years before.

I never told my wife the fearful events which I have just related to you. I told the surgeon who attended me; but he treated the whole adventure as a mere dream born of the fever in my brain. We discussed the question over and over again, until we found that we could discuss it with temper no longer, and then we dropped it. Others may form what conclusions they please -- I know that twenty years ago I was the fourth inside passenger in that Phantom Coach.

Food For Thought

The narrator never told his wife or anybody about the fearful events that occurred with him. Can you say, why? Answer the question briefly in your own words.

An Understanding

Q. 1. What was the name of the narrator in this story? What was his profession and how did he come across the snw covered moor and find a desolate house?
Ans. _____

Q. 2. Why did he feel that the host of the desolate house was very strange? How did he behave with the narrator?
Ans. _____

Q. 3. Who was Jacob and why was he forced to do what the host of the desolate house ordered? What did the host tell the narrator about a horribel crash of a coach?
Ans. _____

Q. 4. The narrator woke up in a hospital having survived a coach crash. What had brought him to the hospital? Was the whole incident a dream or hallucination? Give relevant reasons for your answer.
Ans. _____

Mrs. Zant and the Ghost
~ Wilkie Collins

I

THe course of this narrative describes the return of a *disembodied* spirit to earth, and leads the reader on new and strange ground.

Not in the *obscurity* of midnight, but in the searching light of day, did the *supernatural* influence assert itself. Neither revealed by a vision, nor announced by a voice, it reached mortal knowledge through the sense which is least easily *self-deceived*: the sense that feels.

The record of this event will of necessity produce conflicting impressions. It will raise, in some minds, the doubt which reason asserts; it will invigorate, in other minds, the hope which faith justifies; and it will leave the terrible question of the *destinies* of man, where centuries of vain investigation have left it -- in the dark.

Having only undertaken in the present narrative to lead the way along a succession of events, the writer declines to follow modern examples by *thrusting* himself and his opinions on the public view. He returns to the shadow from which he has emerged, and leaves the opposing forces of *incredulity* and belief to fight the old battle over again, on the old ground.

II

The events happened soon after the first thirty years of the present century had come to an end.

On a fine morning, early in the month of April, a gentleman of middle age (named Rayburn) took his little daughter Lucy out for a walk in the woodland pleasure-ground of Western London, called Kensington Gardens.

The few friends whom he possessed reported of Mr. Rayburn (not unkindly) that he was a *reserved* and *solitary*

Disembodied - *Freed form thj body*
Obscurity - *Uncertainty*
Destinies - *Fate*
Incredulity - *Disbelief, doubt*
Solitary - *Lonely*

man. He might have been more accurately described as a *widower* devoted to his only surviving child. Although he was not more than forty years of age, the one pleasure which made life enjoyable to Lucy's father was offered by Lucy herself.

Playing with her ball, the child ran on to the southern limit of the Gardens, at that part of it which still remains nearest to the old Palace of Kensington. Observing close at hand one of those *spacious* covered seats, called in England "alcoves," Mr. Rayburn was reminded that he had the morning's newspaper in his pocket, and that he might do well to rest and read. At that early hour the place was a *solitude*.

"Go on playing, my dear," he said; "but take care to keep where I can see you."

Lucy tossed up her ball; and Lucy's father opened his newspaper. He had not been reading for more than ten minutes, when he felt a familiar little hand laid on his knee.

"Tired of playing?" he inquired -- with his eyes still on the newspaper.

"I'm frightened, papa."

He looked up directly. The child's pale face *startled* him. He took her on his knee and kissed her.

"You oughtn't to be frightened, Lucy, when I am with you," he said, gently. "What is it?" He looked out of the alcove as he spoke, and saw a little dog among the trees. "Is it the dog?" he asked.

Lucy answered:

"It's not the dog -- it's the lady."

The lady was not visible from the alcove.

"Has she said anything to you?" Mr. Rayburn inquired.

"No."

"What has she done to frighten you?"

The child put her arms round her father's neck.

"*Whisper*, papa," she said; "I'm afraid of her hearing us. I think she's mad."

"Why do you think so, Lucy?"

"She came near to me. I thought she was going to say something. She seemed to be ill."

"Well? And what then?"

Widower - *A man who has lost his wife*
Spacious - *Occupying much space*
Solitude - *Lonely*
Startled - *Very surprised*
Whisper - *Murmur*

"She looked at me."

There, Lucy found herself at a loss how to express what she had to say next -- and took refuge in silence.

"Nothing very wonderful, so far," her father suggested.

"Yes, papa -- but she didn't seem to see me when she looked."

"Well, and what happened then?"

"The lady was frightened -- and that frightened me. I think," the child repeated positively, "she's mad."

It occurred to Mr. Rayburn that the lady might be blind. He rose at once to set the doubt at rest.

"Wait here," he said, "and I'll come back to you."

But Lucy clung to him with both hands; Lucy declared that she was afraid to be by herself. They left the *alcove* together.

The new point of view at once revealed the stranger, leaning against the trunk of a tree. She was dressed in the deep ***mourning*** of a widow. The ***pallor*** of her face, the glassy stare in her eyes, more than accounted for the child's terror -- it excused the alarming conclusion at which she had arrived.

"Go nearer to her," Lucy whispered.

They advanced a few steps. It was now easy to see that the lady was young, and wasted by illness -- but (arriving at a doubtful conclusion perhaps under the present circumstances) apparently possessed of rare personal attractions in happier days. As the father and daughter advanced a little, she discovered them. After some ***hesitation***, she left the tree; approached with an evident intention of speaking; and suddenly paused. A change to astonishment and fear animated her vacant eyes. If it had not been plain before, it was now beyond all doubt that she was not a poor blind creature, deserted and helpless. At the same time, the expression of her face was not easy to understand. She could hardly have looked more amazed and bewildered, if the two strangers who were observing her had suddenly vanished from the place in which they stood.

Mr. Rayburn spoke to her with the utmost kindness of voice and manner.

"I am afraid you are not well," he said. "Is there anything that I can do --"

Alcove - *Any recessed or covered seeluded spot*
Mourning - *Lamenting*
Pallor - *Extreme paleness*
Hesitation - *Reluctance*

The next words were suspended on his lips. It was impossible to *realize* such a state of things; but the strange impression that she had already produced on him was now confirmed. If he could believe his senses, her face did certainly tell him that he was invisible and *inaudible* to the woman whom he had just addressed! She moved slowly away with a heavy sigh, like a person disappointed and distressed. Following her with his eyes, he saw the dog once more -- a little smooth-coated terrier of the ordinary English breed. The dog showed none of the restless activity of his race. With his head down and his tail depressed, he crouched like a creature *paralyzed* by fear. His mistress roused him by a call. He followed her listlessly as she turned away.

After walking a few paces only, she suddenly stood still.

Mr. Rayburn heard her talking to herself.

"Did I feel it again?" she said, as if perplexed by some doubt that awed or grieved her. After a while her arms rose slowly, and opened with a gentle *caressing* action -- an embrace strangely offered to the empty air! "No," she said to herself, sadly, after waiting a moment. "More perhaps when to-morrow comes -- no more to-day." She looked up at the clear blue sky. "The beautiful sunlight! the merciful sunlight!" she murmured. "I should have died if it had happened in the dark."

Once more she called to the dog; and once more she walked slowly away.

"Is she going home, papa?' the child asked.

"We will try and find out," the father answered.

He was by this time convinced that the poor creature was in no condition to be permitted to go out without some one to take care of her. From *motives* of humanity, he was resolved on making the attempt to communicate with her friends.

III

Inaudible - *Incapable of being heard*
Caressing - *Fondling*
Paralysed - *Incativity or inability to act*
Thoroughfare - *Access*
Motives - *Intentions*

The lady left the Gardens by the nearest gate; stopping to lower her veil before she turned into the busy *thoroughfare* which leads to Kensington. Advancing a little way along the High Street, she entered a house of respectable appearance, with a card in one of the windows which announced that apartments were to let.

Mr. Rayburn waited a minute -- then knocked at the door, and asked if he could see the mistress of the house. The servant showed him into a room on the ground floor, neatly but *scantily* furnished. One little white object varied the grim brown *monotony* of the empty table. It was a visiting-card.

With a child's *unceremonious* curiosity Lucy pounced on the card, and spelled the name, letter by letter: "Z, A, N, T," she repeated. "What does that mean?"

Her father looked at the card, as he took it away from her, and put it back on the table. The name was printed, and the address was added in pencil: "Mr. John Zant, Purley's Hotel."

The mistress made her appearance. Mr. Rayburn heartily wished himself out of the house again, the moment he saw her. The ways in which it is possible to cultivate the social virtues are more numerous and more varied than is generally supposed. This lady's way had apparently accustomed her to meet her fellow-creatures on the hard ground of justice without mercy. Something in her eyes, when she looked at Lucy, said: "I wonder whether that child gets punished when she deserves it?"

"Do you wish to see the rooms which I have to let?" she began.

Mr. Rayburn at once stated the object of his visit -- as clearly, as civilly, and as concisely as a man could do it. He was conscious (he added) that he had been guilty perhaps of an act of *intrusion*.

The manner of the mistress of the house showed that she entirely agreed with him. He suggested, however, that his motive might excuse him. The mistress's manner changed, and asserted a difference of opinion.

"I only know the lady whom you mention," she said, "as a person of the highest *respectability*, in delicate health. She has taken my first-floor apartments, with excellent *references*; and she gives remarkably little trouble. I have no claim to interfere with her proceedings, and no reason to doubt that she is capable of taking care of herself."

Mr. Rayburn unwisely attempted to say a word in his own defense.

"Allow me to remind you --" he began.

"Of what, sir?"

Scantily - *Scarcely*
Monotony - *Wearisome routine*
Unceremonious - *Informal*
Intrusion - *An unwelcome visit*
Respectability - *Deserving the respect of other people*
References - *Citations*

"Of what I observed, when I happened to see the lady in Kensington Gardens."

"I am not responsible for what you observed in Kensington Gardens. If your time is of any value, pray don't let me detain you."

Dismissed in those terms, Mr. Rayburn took Lucy's hand and **withdrew**. He had just reached the door, when it was opened from the outer side. The Lady of Kensington Gardens stood before him. In the position which he and his daughter now occupied, their backs were toward the window. Would she remember having seen them for a moment in the Gardens?

"Excuse me for intruding on you," she said to the landlady. "Your servant tells me my brother-in-law called while I was out. He sometimes leaves a message on his card."

She looked for the message, and appeared to be disappointed: there was no writing on the card.

Mr. Rayburn lingered a little in the doorway on the chance of hearing something more. The landlady's **vigilant** eyes discovered him.

"Do you know this gentleman?" she said **maliciously** to her lodger.

"Not that I remember."

Replying in those words, the lady looked at Mr. Rayburn for the first time; and suddenly drew back from him.

"Yes," she said, correcting herself; "I think we met --"

Her embarrassment overpowered her; she could say no more.

Mr. Rayburn **compassionately** finished the sentence for her.

"We met accidentally in Kensington Gardens," he said.

She seemed to be incapable of appreciating the kindness of his motive. After hesitating a little she addressed a proposal to him, which seemed to show distrust of the landlady.

"Will you let me speak to you upstairs in my own rooms?" she asked.

Without waiting for a reply, she led the way to the stairs. Mr. Rayburn and Lucy followed. They were just beginning the ***ascent*** to the first floor, when the ***spiteful*** landlady left the lower room, and called to her lodger over their heads: "Take care what you say to this man, Mrs. Zant! He thinks you're mad."

Withdrew - *To draw back*
Vigilant - *Careful*
Maliciously - *Spiteful*
Compassionately - *Affectionately*
Ascent - *Upward movement*
Spiteful - *Mean, cruel*

Mrs. Zant turned round on the landing, and looked at him. Not a word fell from her lips. She suffered, she feared, in silence. Something in the sad submission of her face touched the springs of *innocent* pity in Lucy's heart. The child burst out crying.

That artless expression of *sympathy* drew Mrs. Zant down the few stairs which separated her from Lucy.

"May I kiss your dear little girl?" she said to Mr. Rayburn. The landlady, standing on the mat below, expressed her opinion of the value of caresses, as compared with a sounder method of treating young persons in tears: "If that child was mine," she remarked, "I would give her something to cry for."

In the meantime, Mrs. Zant led the way to her rooms.

The first words she spoke showed that the landlady had succeeded but too well in *prejudicing* her against Mr. Rayburn.

"Will you let me ask your child," she said to him, "why you think me mad?"

He met this strange request with a firm answer.

"You don't know yet what I really do think. Will you give me a minute's attention?"

"No," she said positively. "The child pities me, I want to speak to the child. What did you see me do in the Gardens, my dear, that surprised you?" Lucy turned uneasily to her father; Mrs. Zant *persisted*. "I first saw you by yourself, and then I saw you with your father," she went on. "When I came nearer to you, did I look very oddly -- as if I didn't see you at all?"

Lucy hesitated again; and Mr. Rayburn *interfered*.

"You are confusing my little girl," he said. "Allow me to answer your questions -- or excuse me if I leave you."

There was something in his look, or in his tone, that mastered her. She put her hand to her head.

"I don't think I'm fit for it," she answered *vacantly*. "My courage has been sorely tried already. If I can get a little rest and sleep, you may find me a different person. I am left a great deal by myself; and I have reasons for trying to compose my mind. Can I see you tomorrow? Or write to you? Where do you live?"

Mr. Rayburn laid his card on the table in silence. She had strongly excited his interest. He honestly desired to be of

Sympathy - *Compassion*
Prejudicing - *Preconception*
Persisted - *Insisted*
Interfered - *Intervened*
Vacantly - *Blankly*

some service to this *forlorn* creature -- abandoned so cruelly, as it seemed, to her own guidance. But he had no authority to exercise, no sort of claim to direct her actions, even if she consented to accept his advice. As a last resource he ventured on an *allusion* to the relative of whom she had spoken downstairs.

"When do you expect to see your brother-in-law again?" he said.

"I don't know," she answered. "I should like to see him -- he is so kind to me."

She turned aside to take leave of Lucy.

"Good-by, my little friend. If you live to grow up, I hope you will never be such a *miserable* woman as I am." She suddenly looked round at Mr. Rayburn. "Have you got a wife at home?" she asked.

"My wife is dead."

"And you have a child to comfort you! Please leave me; you harden my heart. Oh, sir, don't you *understand*? You make me envy you!"

Mr. Rayburn was silent when he and his daughter were out in the street again. Lucy, as became a dutiful child, was silent, too. But there are limits to human endurance -- and Lucy's capacity for self-control gave way at last.

"Are you thinking of the lady, papa?" she said.

He only answered by *nodding* his head. His daughter had *interrupted* him at that critical moment in a man's reflections, when he is on the point of making up his mind. Before they were at home again Mr. Rayburn had arrived at a decision. Mrs. Zant's brother-in-law was evidently ignorant of any serious necessity for his interference -- or he would have made arrangements for immediately repeating his visit. In this state of things, if any evil happened to Mrs. Zant, silence on Mr. Rayburn's part might be indirectly to blame for a serious misfortune. Arriving at that conclusion, he decided upon running the risk of being rudely received, for the second time, by another stranger.

Leaving Lucy under the care of her governess, he went at once to the address that had been written on the visiting-card left at the lodging-house, and sent in his name. A *courteous* message was returned. Mr. John Zant was at home, and would be happy to see him.

Forlorn - *Desolate*
Allusion - *A casual reference*
Miserable - *Wretchedly*
Endurance - *For beardnee*
Nodding - *To make a slight, quick downward movment*
Interrupted - *To break off*
Courteous - *Well mannered*

IV

Mr. Rayburn was shown into one of the private sitting-rooms of the hotel.

He observed that the *customary* position of the furniture in a room had been, in some respects, altered. An armchair, a side-table, and a footstool had all been removed to one of the windows, and had been placed as close as possible to the light. On the table lay a large open roll of morocco leather, containing rows of elegant little instruments in steel and ivory. Waiting by the table, stood Mr. John Zant. He said "Good-morning" in a bass voice, so profound and so melodious that those two commonplace words assumed a new importance, coming from his lips. His personal appearance was in harmony with his magnificent voice -- he was a tall, finely-made man of dark *complexion*; with big brilliant black eyes, and a noble curling beard, which hid the whole lower part of his face. Having bowed with a happy mingling of dignity and politeness, the *conventional* side of this gentleman's character suddenly vanished; and a crazy side, to all appearance, took its place. He dropped on his knees in front of the footstool. Had he forgotten to say his prayers that morning, and was he in such a hurry to remedy the fault that he had no time to spare for consulting appearances? The doubt had hardly suggested itself, before it was set at rest in a most unexpected manner. Mr. Zant looked at his visitor with a bland smile, and said:

"Please let me see your feet."

For the moment, Mr. Rayburn lost his presence of mind. He looked at the instruments on the side-table. "Are you a corn-cutter?" was all he could say.

"Excuse me, sir, " returned the polite operator, "the term you use is quite *obsolete* in our profession." He rose from his knees, and added modestly: "I am a Chiropodist."

"I beg your pardon."

"Don't mention it! You are not, I imagine, in want of my professional services. To what motive may I *attribute* the honor of your visit?"

By this time Mr. Rayburn had recovered himself.

Customary - *Habitual*
Complexion - *The natural colour*
Conventional - *Customary*
Absolete - *Outdated*
Attribute - *Impute, ascribe*

"I have come here," he answered, "under circumstances which require apology as well as explanation." Mr. Zant's highly polished manner *betrayed* signs of alarm; his suspicions pointed to a *formidable* conclusion -- a conclusion that shook him to the innermost recesses of the pocket in which he kept his money.

"The numerous demands on me --" he began.

Mr. Rayburn smiled.

"Make your mind easy," he replied. "I don't want money. My object is to speak with you on the subject of a lady who is a relation of yours."

"My sister-in-law!" Mr. Zant exclaimed. "Pray take a seat."

Doubting if he had chosen a convenient time for his visit, Mr. Rayburn hesitated.

"Am I likely to be in the way of persons who wish to consult you?" he asked.

"Certainly not. My morning hours of attendance on my clients are from eleven to one." The clock on the mantelpiece struck the quarter-past one as he spoke. "I hope you don't bring me bad news?" he said, very *earnestly*. "When I called on Mrs. Zant this morning, I heard that she had gone out for a walk. Is it indiscreet to ask how you became acquainted with her?"

Mr. Rayburn at once mentioned what he had seen and heard in Kensington Gardens; not forgetting to add a few words, which described his interview afterward with Mrs. Zant.

The lady's brother-in-law listened with an interest and sympathy, which offered the strongest possible contrast to the *unprovoked rudeness* of the mistress of the lodging-house. He declared that he could only do justice to his sense of obligation by following Mr. Rayburn's example, and expressing himself as frankly as if he had been speaking to an old friend.

"The sad story of my sister-in-law's life," he said, "will, I think, explain certain things which must have naturally perplexed you. My brother was introduced to her at the house of an Australian gentleman, on a visit to England. She was then employed as governess to his daughters. So sincere was the regard felt for her by the family that the parents had, at the entreaty of their children, asked her to *accompany* them

Betrayed - *To be unfaithful*
Formidable - *Appalling*
Earnestly - *Trully*
Unprovoked - *Not nagry on anything done or said*
Rudeness - *Harshness*
Accompany - *To escort, go along*

when they returned to the Colony. The governess thankfully accepted the *proposal*."

"Had she no relations in England?" Mr. Rayburn asked.

"She was literally alone in the world, sir. When I tell you that she had been brought up in the Foundling Hospital, you will understand what I mean. Oh, there is no romance in my sister-in-law's story! She never has known, or will know, who her parents were or why they deserted her. The happiest moment in her life was the moment when she and my brother first met. It was an instance, on both sides, of love at first sight. Though not a rich man, my brother had earned a sufficient income in *mercantile* pursuits. His character spoke for itself. In a word, he altered all the poor girl's prospects, as we then hoped and believed, for the better. Her employers *deferred* their return to Australia, so that she might be married from their house. After a happy life of a few weeks only --"

His voice failed him; he *paused*, and turned his face from the light.

"Pardon me," he said; "I am not able, even yet, to speak composedly of my brother's death. Let me only say that the poor young wife was a widow, before the happy days of the honeymoon were over. That dreadful *calamity* struck her down. Before my brother had been *committed* to the grave, her life was in danger from brain-fever."

Those words placed in a new light Mr. Rayburn's first fear that her intellect might be deranged. Looking at him attentively, Mr. Zant seemed to understand what was passing in the mind of his guest.

"No!" he said. "If the opinions of the medical men are to be trusted, the result of the illness is injury to her physical strength -- not injury to her mind. I have observed in her, no doubt, a certain *waywardness* of temper since her illness; but that is a trifle. As an example of what I mean, I may tell you that I invited her, on her recovery, to pay me a visit. My house is not in London -- the air doesn't agree with me -- my place of residence is at St. Sallins-on-Sea. I am not myself a married man; but my excellent housekeeper would have received Mrs. Zant with the utmost kindness. She was resolved -- *obstinately* resolved, poor thing -- to remain in London. It is needless to say that, in her *melancholy* position, I am attentive to her slightest wishes. I took a lodging for her;

Proposal - *Plan, scheme*
Mercantile - *Commercial*
Deferred - *Postponed*
Calamity - *Disaster*
Waywardness - *Disobedient*
Obstinately - *Stubbornly*
Melancholy - *Sadness*

and, at her special request, I chose a house which was near Kensington Gardens.

"Is there any association with the Gardens which led Mrs. Zant to make that request?"

"Some association, I believe, with the memory of her husband. By the way, I wish to be sure of finding her at home, when I call to-morrow. Did you say (in the course of your interesting statement) that she intended -- as you supposed -- to return to Kensington Gardens to-morrow? Or has my memory *deceived* me?"

"Your memory is perfectly accurate."

"Thank you. I confess I am not only *distressed* by what you have told me of Mrs. Zant -- I am at a loss to know how to act for the best. My only idea, at present, is to try change of air and scene. What do you think yourself?"

"I think you are right."

Mr. Zant still *hesitated*.

"It would not be easy for me, just now," he said, "to leave my patients and take her abroad."

The obvious reply to this occurred to Mr. Rayburn. A man of larger worldly experience might have felt certain suspicions, and might have remained silent. Mr. Rayburn spoke.

"Why not renew your invitation and take her to your house at the seaside?" he said.

In the *perplexed* state of Mr. Zant's mind, this plain course of action had apparently failed to present itself. His gloomy face brightened directly.

"The very thing!" he said. "I will certainly take your advice. If the air of St. Sallins does nothing else, it will improve her health and help her to recover her good looks. Did she strike you as having been (in happier days) a pretty woman?"

This was a strangely familiar question to ask -- almost an *indelicate* question, under the circumstances A certain furtive expression in Mr. Zant's fine dark eyes seemed to imply that it had been put with a purpose. Was it possible that he suspected Mr. Rayburn's interest in his sister-in-law to be inspired by any motive which was not perfectly unselfish and perfectly pure? To arrive at such a conclusion as this might be to judge *hastily* and cruelly of a man who was perhaps only guilty of a want of *delicacy* of feeling. Mr. Rayburn honestly did his best

---

Deceived - *Misled*
Hesitated - *To be reluctant*
Perplexed - *Astonished*
Indelicate - *Unrefined*
Hastily - *Quickly*
Delicacy - *Fineness of quality*

to assume the charitable point of view. At the same time, it is not to be denied that his words, when he answered, were carefully guarded, and that he rose to take his leave.

Mr. John Zant *hospitably protested*.

"Why are you in such a hurry? Must you really go? I shall have the honor of returning your visit to-morrow, when I have made arrangements to profit by that excellent suggestion of yours. Good-by. God bless you."

He held out his hand: a hand with a smooth surface and a tawny color, that *fervently squeezed* the fingers of a departing friend. "Is that man a scoundrel?" was Mr. Rayburn's first thought, after he had left the hotel. His moral sense set all hesitation at rest -- and answered: "You're a fool if you doubt it."

V

Disturbed by *presentiments*, Mr. Rayburn returned to his house on foot, by way of trying what exercise would do toward composing his mind.

The experiment failed. He went upstairs and played with Lucy; he drank an extra glass of wine at dinner; he took the child and her governess to a circus in the evening; he ate a little supper, fortified by another glass of wine, before he went to bed -- and still those vague *forebodings* of evil persisted in torturing him. Looking back through his past life, he asked himself if any woman (his late wife of course excepted!) had ever taken the predominant place in his thoughts which Mrs. Zant had assumed -- without any *discernible* reason to account for it? If he had ventured to answer his own question, the reply would have been: Never!

All the next day he waited at home, in expectation of Mr. John Zant's promised visit, and waited in vain.

Toward evening the parlor-maid appeared at the family tea-table, and presented to her master an unusually large envelope sealed with black wax, and addressed in a strange handwriting. The absence of stamp and postmark showed that it had been left at the house by a messenger.

"Who brought this?" Mr. Rayburn asked.

"A lady, sir -- in deep mourning."

"Did she leave any message?"

Hospitably - *Welcoming*
Protested - *Retaliated*
Fervently - *Passionate*
Squeezed - *Compressed*
Presentiments - *Premonitions*
Foreboding - *Prediction*
Discernible - *Perceptible*

"No, sir."

Having drawn the *inevitable* conclusion, Mr. Rayburn shut himself up in his library. He was afraid of Lucy's curiosity and Lucy's questions, if he read Mrs. Zant's letter in his daughter's presence.

Looking at the open envelope after he had taken out the leaves of writing which it contained, he noticed these lines traced inside the cover:

"My one excuse for troubling you, when I might have consulted my brother-in-law, will be found in the pages which I inclose. To speak plainly, you have been led to fear that I am not in my right senses. For this very reason, I now appeal to you. Your *dreadful* doubt of me, sir, is my doubt too. Read what I have written about myself -- and then tell me, I entreat you, which I am: A person who has been the object of a supernatural *revelation*? or an unfortunate creature who is only fit for imprisonment in a mad-house?"

Mr. Rayburn opened the manuscript. With steady attention, which soon quickened to breathless interest, he read what follows:

VI - THE LADY'S MANUSCRIPT

Yesterday morning the sun shone in a clear blue sky -- after a succession of cloudy days, counting from the first of the month.

The radiant light had its *animating* effect on my poor spirits. I had passed the night more peacefully than usual; undisturbed by the dream, so cruelly familiar to me, that my lost husband is still living -- the dream from which I always wake in tears. Never, since the dark days of my sorrow, have I been so little troubled by the *self-tormenting fancies* and fears which beset miserable women, as when I left the house, and turned my steps toward Kensington Gardens -- for the first time since my husband's death.

Attended by my only companion, the little dog who had been his favourite as well as mine, I went to the quiet corner of the Gardens which is nearest to Kensington.

On that soft grass, under the shade of those grand trees, we had *loitered* together in the days of our *betrothal*. It was his favorite walk; and he had taken me to see it in the early

Inevitable - *Destined*
Dreadful - *Fearful*
Revelation -
Disclosure

days of our acquaintance. There, he had first asked me to be his wife. There, we had felt the *rapture* of our first kiss. It was surely natural that I should wish to see once more a place sacred to such memories as these? I am only twenty-three years old; I have no child to comfort me, no companion of my own age, nothing to love but the *dumb* creature who is so faithfully fond of me.

I went to the tree under which we stood, when my dear one's eyes told his love before he could utter it in words. The sun of that vanished day shone on me again; it was the same noontide hour; the same solitude was around me. I had feared the first effect of the *dreadful* contrast between past and present. No! I was quiet and resigned. My thoughts, rising higher than earth, dwelt on the better life beyond the grave. Some tears came into my eyes. But I was not unhappy. My memory of all that happened may be trusted, even in trifles which relate only to myself -- I was not unhappy.

The first object that I saw, when my eyes were clear again, was the dog. He crouched a few paces away from me, trembling pitiably, but uttering no cry. What had caused the fear that overpowered him?

I was soon to know.

I called to the dog; he remained *immovable* -- conscious of some mysterious coming thing that held him *spellbound*. I tried to go to the poor creature, and fondle and comfort him.

At the first step forward that I took, something stopped me.

It was not to be seen, and not to be heard. It stopped me.

The still figure of the dog disappeared from my view: the lonely scene around me disappeared -- excepting the light from heaven, the tree that sheltered me, and the grass in front of me. A sense of *unutterable* expectation kept my eyes riveted on the grass. Suddenly, I saw its myriad blades rise erect and shivering. The fear came to me of something passing over them with the invisible swiftness of the wind. The shivering advanced. It was all round me. It crept into the leaves of the tree over my head; they *shuddered*, without a sound to tell of their agitation; their pleasant natural *rustling* was struck dumb. The song of the birds had ceased. The cries of the water-fowl on the pond were heard no more. There was a dreadful silence.

Spellbound - *Awestruck, enthralled*
Unutterable - *That cannot be spoken*
Shuddered - *Shivered*
Rustling - *Rubbing gently*

But the lovely sunshine poured down on me, as brightly as ever.

In that dazzling light, in that fearful silence, I felt an Invisible Presence near me. It touched me gently.

At the touch, my heart throbbed with an overwhelming joy. *Exquisite* pleasure *thrilled* through every nerve in my body. I knew him! From the unseen world -- himself unseen -- he had returned to me. Oh, I knew him!

And yet, my helpless *mortality* longed for a sign that might give me assurance of the truth. The *yearning* in me shaped itself into words. I tried to utter the words. I would have said, if I could have spoken: "Oh, my angel, give me a token that it is You!" But I was like a person struck dumb -- I could only think it.

The Invisible Presence read my thought. I felt my lips touched, as my husband's lips used to touch them when he kissed me. And that was my answer. A thought came to me again. I would have said, if I could have spoken: "Are you here to take me to the better world?"

I waited. Nothing that I could feel touched me.

I was conscious of thinking once more. I would have said, if I could have spoken: "Are you here to protect me?"

I felt myself held in a gentle embrace, as my husband's arms used to hold me when he pressed me to his breast. And that was my answer.

The touch that was like the touch of his lips, lingered and was lost; the clasp that was like the clasp of his arms, pressed me and fell away. The garden-scene resumed its natural aspect. I saw a human creature near, a lovely little girl looking at me.

At that moment, when I was my own lonely self again, the sight of the child soothed and attracted me. I advanced, *intending* to speak to her. To my horror I suddenly ceased to see her. She disappeared as if I had been stricken blind.

And yet I could see the landscape round me; I could see the heaven above me. A time passed -- only a few minutes, as I thought -- and the child became visible to me again; walking hand-in-hand with her father. I approached them; I was close enough to see that they were looking at me with pity and surprise. My *impulse* was to ask if they saw anything strange

Exquisite - *Extraordinary*
Thrilled - *Excited*
Mortality - *The number of deaths in a given period*
Intending - *Designing*
Impulse - *A sudden desire urge*

in my face or my manner. Before I could speak, the horrible wonder happened again. They vanished from my view.

Was the Invisible Presence still near? Was it passing between me and my fellow-mortals; *forbidding* communication, in that place and at that time?

It must have been so. When I turned away in my ignorance, with a heavy heart, the dreadful *blankness* which had twice shut out from me the beings of my own race, was not between me and my dog. The poor little creature filled me with pity; I called him to me. He moved at the sound of my voice, and followed me *languidly*; not quite awakened yet from the trance of terror that had possessed him.

Before I had retired by more than a few steps, I thought I was conscious of the Presence again. I held out my longing arms to it. I waited in the hope of a touch to tell me that I might return. Perhaps I was answered by indirect means? I only know that a *resolution* to return to the same place, at the same hour, came to me, and quieted my mind.

The morning of the next day was dull and cloudy; but the rain held off. I set forth again to the Gardens.

My dog ran on before me into the street -- and stopped: waiting to see in which direction I might lead the way. When I turned toward the Gardens, he dropped behind me. In a little while I looked back. He was following me no longer; he stood irresolute. I called to him. He advanced a few steps -- hesitated -- and ran back to the house.

I went on by myself. Shall I confess my *superstition*? I thought the dog's desertion of me a bad omen.

Arrived at the tree, I placed myself under it. The minutes followed each other uneventfully. The cloudy sky darkened. The dull surface of the grass showed no shuddering consciousness of an *unearthly* creature passing over it.

I still waited, with an obstinacy which was fast becoming the *obstinacy* of despair. How long an interval *elapsed*, while I kept watch on the ground before me, I am not able to say. I only know that a change came.

Under the dull gray light I saw the grass move -- but not as it had moved, on the day before. It shrivelled as if a flame had scorched it. No flame appeared. The brown underlying earth showed itself winding onward in a thin strip -- which

Forbidding - *Threatening*
Languidly - *Sluggishly*
Resolution - *Pass by*
Superstition - *Belief, notion*
Elapsed - *Determination*

might have been a footpath traced in fire. It frightened me. I longed for the protection of the Invisible Presence. I prayed for a warning of it, if danger was near.

A touch answered me. It was as if a hand unseen had taken my hand -- had raised it, little by little -- had left it, pointing to the thin brown path that wound toward me under the shrivelled blades of grass.

I looked to the far end of the path.

The unseen hand closed on my hand with a warning pressure: the *revelation* of the coming danger was near me -- I waited for it. I saw it.

The figure of a man appeared, advancing toward me along the thin brown path. I looked in his face as he came nearer. It showed me *dimly* the face of my husband's brother -- John Zant.

The consciousness of myself as a living creature left me. I knew nothing; I felt nothing. I was dead.

When the torture of revival made me open my eyes, I found myself on the grass. Gentle hands raised my head, at the moment when I recovered my senses. Who had brought me to life again? Who was taking care of me?

I looked upward, and saw -- bending over me -- John Zant.

VII

There, the manuscript ended.

Some lines had been added on the last page; but they had been so carefully erased as to be illegible. These words of explanation appeared below the canceled sentences:

"I had begun to write the little that remains to be told, when it struck me that I might, *unintentionally*, be exercising an unfair influence on your opinion. Let me only remind you that I believe absolutely in the supernatural revelation which I have endeavored to describe. Remember this -- and decide for me what I dare not decide for myself."

There was no serious obstacle in the way of compliance with this request.

Judged from the point of view of the materialist, Mrs. Zant might no doubt be the victim of illusions (produced

Revelation -
Disclosure
Dimly - *Not brightly*
Unintentionally -
Not deliberately

by a diseased state of the nervous system), which have been known to exist -- as in the celebrated case of the book-seller, Nicolai, of Berlin -- without being accompanied by derangement of the intellectual powers. But Mr. Rayburn was not asked to solve any such *intricate* problem as this. He had been merely instructed to read the manuscript, and to say what impression it had left on him of the mental condition of the writer; whose doubt of herself had been, in all probability, first suggested by remembrance of the illness from which she had suffered -- brain-fever.

Under these circumstances, there could be little difficulty in forming an opinion. The memory which had recalled, and the judgement which had arranged, the succession of events related in the narrative, revealed a mind in full possession of its resources.

Having satisfied himself so far, Mr. Rayburn abstained from considering the more serious question suggested by what he had read.

At any time his habits of life and his ways of thinking would have *rendered* him unfit to weigh the arguments, which assert or deny supernatural revelation among the creatures of earth. But his mind was now so disturbed by the startling record of experience which he had just read, that he was only conscious of feeling certain impressions -- without possessing the capacity to reflect on them. That his anxiety on Mrs. Zant's account had been increased, and that his doubts of Mr. John Zant had been encouraged, were the only practical results of the confidence placed in him of which he was thus far aware. In the ordinary *exigencies* of life a man of hesitating *disposition*, his interest in Mrs. Zant's welfare, and his desire to discover what had passed between her brother-in-law and herself, after their meeting in the Gardens, urged him into instant action. In half an hour more, he had arrived at her lodgings. He was at once admitted.

VIII

Mrs. Zant was alone, in an *imperfectly* lighted room.

"I hope you will excuse the bad light," she said; "my head has been burning as if the fever had come back again. Oh,

Intricate - *Delicate*
Rendered - *Performed*
Disposition - *Temperament*
Exigencies - *Urgency emergency*
Imperfectly - *Not properly*

don't go away! After what I have suffered, you don't know how dreadful it is to be alone."

The tone of her voice told him that she had been crying. He at once tried the best means of setting the poor lady at ease, by telling her of the conclusion at which he had arrived, after reading her manuscript. The happy result showed itself instantly: her face brightened, her manner changed; she was eager to hear more.

"Have I produced any other impression on you?" she asked.

He understood the *allusion*. Expressing sincere respect for her own convictions, he told her honestly that he was not prepared to enter on the *obscure* and terrible question of supernatural *interposition*. *Grateful* for the tone in which he had answered her, she wisely and delicately changed the subject.

"I must speak to you of my brother-in-law," she said. "He has told me of your visit; and I am anxious to know what you think of him. Do you like Mr. John Zant?"

Mr. Rayburn hesitated.

The careworn look appeared again in her face. "If you had felt as kindly towards him as he feels toward you," she said, "I might have gone to St. Sallins with a lighter heart."

Mr. Rayburn thought of the supernatural appearances, described at the close of her narrative. "You believe in that terrible warning," he *remonstrated*; "and yet, you go to your brother-in-law's house!"

"I believe," she answered, "in the spirit of the man who loved me in the days of his earthly *bondage*. I am under his protection. What have I to do but to cast away my fears, and to wait in faith and hope? It might have helped my resolution if a friend had been near to encourage me." She paused and smiled sadly. "I must remember," she resumed, "that your way of understanding my position is not my way. I ought to have told you that Mr. John Zant feels needless anxiety about my health. He declares that he will not lose sight of me until his mind is at ease. It is useless to attempt to alter his opinion. He says my nerves are *shattered* -- and who that sees me can doubt it? He tells me that my only chance of getting better is to try change of air and perfect repose -- how can I *contradict* him? He reminds me that I have no relation but himself, and no house open to me but his own -- and God knows he is right!"

Allusion - *Elusion*
Interposition - *Opposing any government action*
Remonstrated - *To plead in protest*
Bondage - *Slavery*
Contradict - *Oppose*

She said those last words in **accents** of melancholy resignation, which grieved the good man whose one merciful purpose was to serve and **console** her. He spoke impulsively with the freedom of an old friend

"I want to know more of you and Mr. John Zant than I know now," he said. "My motive is a better one than mere curiosity. Do you believe that I feel a sincere interest in you?"

"With my whole heart."

That reply encouraged him to proceed with what he had to say. "When you recovered from your fainting-fit," he began, "Mr. John Zant asked questions, of course?"

"He asked what could possibly have happened, in such a quiet place as Kensington Gardens, to make me faint."

"And how did you answer?"

"Answer? I couldn't even look at him!"

"You said nothing?"

"Nothing. I don't know what he thought of me; he might have been surprised, or he might have been **offended**."

"Is he easily **offended**?" Mr. Rayburn asked.

"Not in my experience of him."

"Do you mean your experience of him before your illness?"

"Yes. Since my recovery, his engagements with country patients have kept him away from London. I have not seen him since he took these lodgings for me. But he is always **considerate**. He has written more than once to beg that I will not think him neglectful, and to tell me (what I knew already through my poor husband) that he has no money of his own, and must live by his profession."

"In your husband's lifetime, were the two brothers on good terms?"

"Always. The one **complaint** I ever heard my husband make of John Zant was that he didn't come to see us often enough, after our marriage. Is there some wickedness in him which we have never suspected? It may be -- but how can it be? I have every reason to be grateful to the man against whom I have been supernaturally warned! His conduct to me has been always perfect. I can't tell you what I owe to his influence in quieting my mind, when a dreadful doubt arose about my husband's death."

Conslole - *Comfort*
Offended - *Insulted*
Considerate - *Thoughtful*
Complaint - *Resentment*

"Do you mean doubt if he died a natural death?"

"Oh, no! no! He was dying of rapid *consumption* -- but his sudden death took the doctors by surprise. One of them thought that he might have taken an overdose of his sleeping drops, by mistake. The other disputed this conclusion, or there might have been an *inquest* in the house. Oh, don't speak of it any more! Let us talk of something else. Tell me when I shall see you again."

"I hardly know. When do you and your brother-in-law leave London?"

"To-morrow." She looked at Mr. Rayburn with a piteous *entreaty* in her eyes; she said, timidly: "Do you ever go to the seaside, and take your dear little girl with you?"

The request, at which she had only dared to hint, touched on the idea which was at that moment in Mr. Rayburn's mind. *Interpreted* by his strong prejudice against John Zant, what she had said of her brother-in-law filled him with forebodings of peril to herself; all the more powerful in their influence, for this reason -- that he shrank from distinctly realizing them. If another person had been present at the interview, and had said to him afterward: "That man's reluctance to visit his sister-in-law, while her husband was living, is associated with a secret sense of guilt which her innocence cannot even imagine: he, and he alone, knows the cause of her husband's sudden death: his *feigned* anxiety about her health is adopted as the safest means of enticing her into his house -- if those *formidable* conclusions had been urged on Mr. Rayburn, he would have felt it his duty to reject them, as unjustifiable aspersions on an absent man. And yet, when he took leave that evening of Mrs. Zant, he had *pledged* himself to give Lucy a holiday at the seaside: and he had said, without *blushing*, that the child really deserved it, as a reward for general good conduct and attention to her lessons!

IX

Three days later, the father and daughter arrived toward evening at St. Sallins-on-Sea. They found Mrs. Zant at the station.

The poor woman's joy, on seeing them, expressed itself like the joy of a child. "Oh, I am so glad! so glad!" was all

Consumption - *Utilisation*
Inquest - *Legal or judicial inquiry*
Entreaty - *Plea, supplication*
Interpreted - *Explained*
Feigned - *Pretended*
Pledged - *Promised*

she could say when they met. Lucy was half-smothered with kisses, and was made supremely happy by a present of the finest doll she had ever possessed. Mrs. Zant accompanied her friends to the rooms which had been secured at the hotel. She was able to speak *confidentially* to Mr. Rayburn, while Lucy was in the balcony *hugging* her doll, and looking at the sea.

The one event that had happened during Mrs. Zant's short residence at St. Sallins was the departure of her brother-in-law that morning, for London. He had been called away to operate on the feet of a wealthy patient who knew the value of his time: his housekeeper expected that he would return to dinner.

As to his conduct toward Mrs. Zant, he was not only as attentive as ever -- he was almost *oppressively* affectionate in his language and manner. There was no service that a man could render which he had not eagerly offered to her. He declared that he already perceived an improvement in her health; he congratulated her on having decided to stay in his house; and (as a proof, perhaps, of his sincerity) he had repeatedly pressed her hand. "Have you any idea what all this means?" she said, simply.

Mr. Rayburn kept his idea to himself. He professed ignorance; and asked next what sort of person the housekeeper was.

Mrs. Zant shook her head ominously.

"Such a strange creature," she said, "and in the habit of taking such liberties that I begin to be afraid she is a little crazy."

"Is she an old woman?"

"No -- only middle-aged. This morning, after her master had left the house, she actually asked me what I thought of my brother-in-law! I told her, as coldly as possible, that I thought he was very kind. She was quite insensible to the tone in which I had spoken; she went on from bad to worse. "Do you call him the sort of man who would take the fancy of a young woman?" was her next question. She actually looked at me (I might have been wrong; and I hope I was) as if the "young woman" she had in her mind was myself! I said: "I don't think of such things, and I don't talk about them." Still, she was not in the least *discouraged*; she made a personal remark next: "Excuse me -- but you do look *wretchedly* pale." I thought she seemed to enjoy the defect in my *complexion*; I really believe it raised me in her estimation. "We shall get on better in time," she said; "I am

Confidentially - *Secretly*
Hugging - *Clasping*
Oppressively - *Distressingly*
Discouraged - *To deprive*
Wretchedly - *Pitifully*
Complexion - *Natural skin colour*

beginning to like you." She walked out humming a tune. Don't you agree with me? Don't you think she's crazy?"

"I can hardly give an opinion until I have seen her. Does she look as if she might have been a pretty woman at one time of her life?"

"Not the sort of pretty woman whom I admire!"

Mr. Rayburn smiled. "I was thinking," he resumed, "that this person's odd conduct may perhaps be accounted for. She is probably jealous of any young lady who is invited to her master's house -- and (till she noticed your complexion) she began by being jealous of you."

Innocently at a loss to understand how she could become an object of the housekeeper's jealousy, Mrs. Zant looked at Mr. Rayburn in astonishment. Before she could give expression to her feeling of surprise, there was an interruption -- a welcome *interruption*. A waiter entered the room, and announced a visitor; described as "a gentleman."

Mrs. Zant at once rose to retire.

"Who is the gentleman?" Mr. Rayburn asked -- detaining Mrs. Zant as he spoke.

A voice which they both recognised answered *gayly*, from the outer side of the door:

"A friend from London."

X

"Welcome to St. Sallins! " cried Mr. John Zant. "I knew that you were expected, my dear sir, and I took my chance at finding you at the hotel." He turned to his sister-in-law, and kissed her hand with an *elaborate gallantry* worthy of Sir Charles Grandison himself. "When I reached home, my dear, and heard that you had gone out, I guessed that your object was to receive our excellent friend. You have not felt lonely while I have been away? That's right! that's right!" he looked toward the balcony, and discovered Lucy at the open window, *staring* at the magnificent stranger. "Your little daughter, Mr. Rayburn? Dear child! Come and kiss me."

Lucy answered in one positive word: "No."

Mr. John Zant was not easily discouraged.

Interruption - *Disturbance*
Gayly - *happily*
Elaborate - *Detailed*
Gallantry - *Daring*
Staring - *Gazing*

Show me your doll, darling," he said. "Sit on my knee."

Lucy answered in two positive words --"I won't."

Her father approached the window to ***administer*** the necessary ***reproof***. Mr. John Zant interfered in the cause of mercy with his best grace. He held up his hands in cordial entreaty. "Dear Mr. Rayburn! The fairies are sometimes shy; and this little fairy doesn't take to strangers at first sight. Dear child! All in good time. And what stay do you make at St. Sallins? May we hope that our poor attractions will tempt you to prolong your visit?"

He put his flattering little question with an ease of manner which was rather too plainly assumed; and he looked at Mr. Rayburn with a watchfulness which appeared to attach undue importance to the reply. When he said: "What stay do you make at St. Sallins?" did he really mean: "How soon do you leave us?" Inclining to adopt this conclusion, Mr. Rayburn answered ***cautiously*** that his stay at the seaside would depend on circumstances. Mr. John Zant looked at his sister-in-law, sitting silent in a corner with Lucy on her lap. "Exert your attractions," he said; "make the circumstances ***agreeable*** to our good friend. Will you dine with us to-day, my dear sir, and bring your little fairy with you?"

Lucy was far from receiving this ***complimentary allusion*** in the spirit in which it had been offered. "I'm not a fairy," she declared. "I'm a child."

"And a naughty child," her father added, with all the severity that he could assume.

"I can't help it, papa; the man with the big beard puts me out."

The man with the big beard was amused -- ***amiably***, paternally amused -- by Lucy's plain speaking. He repeated his invitation to dinner; and he did his best to look disappointed when Mr. Rayburn made the necessary excuses.

"Another day," he said (without, however, fixing the day). "I think you will find my house comfortable. My housekeeper may perhaps be ***eccentric*** -- but in all essentials a woman in a thousand. Do you feel the change from London already? Our air at St. Sallins is really worthy of its reputation. Invalids who come here are cured as if by magic. What do you think of Mrs. Zant? How does she look?"

Reproof - *Refuke*
Cautiously - *Carefully*
Allusion - *Casual*
Amiably - *Friendly*
Eccentric - *Lunatic reference*

Mr. Rayburn was evidently expected to say that she looked better. He said it. Mr. John Zant seemed to have *anticipated* a stronger expression of opinion.

"Surprisingly better!" he pronounced. "Infinitely better! We ought both to be grateful. Pray believe that we are grateful."

"If you mean grateful to me," Mr. Rayburn remarked, "I don't quite understand --"

"You don't quite understand? Is it possible that you have forgotten our conversation when I first had the honor of receiving you? Look at Mrs. Zant again."

Mr. Rayburn looked; and Mrs. Zant's brother-in-law explained himself.

"You notice the return of her colour, the healthy brightness of her eyes. (No, my dear, I am not paying you idle *compliments*; I am stating plain facts.) For that happy result, Mr. Rayburn, we are *indebted* to you."

"Surely not?"

"Surely yes! It was at your valuable suggestion that I thought of inviting my sister-in-law to visit me at St. Sallins. Ah, you remember it now. Forgive me if I look at my watch; the dinner hour is on my mind. Not, as your dear little daughter there seems to think, because I am greedy, but because I am always punctual, in justice to the cook. Shall we see you to-morrow? Call early, and you will find us at home."

He gave Mrs. Zant his arm, and bowed and smiled, and kissed his hand to Lucy, and left the room. Recalling their interview at the hotel in London, Mr. Rayburn now understood John Zant's object (on that occasion) in *assuming* the character of a helpless man in need of a sensible suggestion. If Mrs. Zant's residence under his roof became associated with evil consequences, he could declare that she would never have entered the house but for Mr. Rayburn's advice.

With the next day came the hateful necessity of returning this man's visit.

Mr. Rayburn was placed between two alternatives. In Mrs. Zant's interests he must remain, no matter at what sacrifice of his own *inclinations*, on good terms with her brother-in-law -- or he must return to London, and leave the poor woman to her fate. His choice, it is needless to say, was never a matter of doubt. He called at the house, and did his innocent best -- without in the least *deceiving* Mr. John Zant

Anticipated - *To foresee*
Compliments - *Praises*
Indebted - *Grateful*
Assuming - *Presumptuous*
Deceiving - *Misleading*

-- to make himself agreeable during the short duration of his visit. **Descending** the stairs on his way out, accompanied by Mrs. Zant, he was surprised to see a middle-aged woman in the hall, who looked as if she was waiting there expressly to attract notice.

"The housekeeper," Mrs. Zant whispered. "She is impudent enough to try to make acquaintance with you."

This was exactly what the housekeeper was waiting in the hall to do.

"I hope you like our watering-place, sir," she began. "If I can be of service to you, pray command me. Any friend of this lady's has a claim on me -- and you are an old friend, no doubt. I am only the housekeeper; but I presume to take a sincere interest in Mrs. Zant; and I am indeed glad to see you here. We none of us know -- do we? -- how soon we may want a friend. No offense, I hope? Thank you, sir. Good-morning."

There was nothing in the woman's eyes which indicated an unsettled mind; nothing in the appearance of her lips which suggested habits of *intoxication*. That her strange **outburst** of familiarity proceeded from some strong motive seemed to be more than probable. Putting together what Mrs. Zant had already told him, and what he had himself observed, Mr. Rayburn suspected that the motive might be found in the housekeeper's jealousy of her master.

XI

Reflecting in the **solitude** of his own room, Mr. Rayburn felt that the one *prudent* course to take would be to persuade Mrs. Zant to leave St. Sallins. He tried to prepare her for this strong proceeding, when she came the next day to take Lucy out for a walk.

"If you still regret having forced yourself to accept your brother-in-law's invitation," was all he *ventured* to say, "don't forget that you are perfect mistress of your own actions. You have only to come to me at the hotel, and I will take you back to London by the next train."

She positively refused to entertain the idea.

"I should be a thankless creature, indeed," she said, "if I accepted your proposal. Do you think I am ungrateful

Descending - *To move downwards*
Intoxication - *Poisoning*
Outburst - *Outbreak*
Prudent - *Wise*
Ventured - *To take the risk of, to embark upon*

enough to involve you in a personal quarrel with John Zant? No! If I find myself forced to leave the house, I will go away alone."

There was no moving her from this *resolution*. When she and Lucy had gone out together, Mr. Rayburn remained at the hotel, with a mind ill at ease. A man of *readier* mental resources might have felt at a loss how to act for the best, in the emergency that now *confronted* him. While he was still as far as ever from arriving at a decision, some person knocked at the door.

Had Mrs. Zant returned? He looked up as the door was opened, and saw to his astonishment -- Mr. John Zant's housekeeper.

"Don't let me alarm you, sir," the woman said. "Mrs. Zant has been taken a little faint, at the door of our house. My master is attending to her."

"Where is the child?" Mr. Rayburn asked.

"I was bringing her back to you, sir, when we met a lady and her little girl at the door of the hotel. They were on their way to the beach -- and Miss Lucy begged hard to be allowed to go with them. The lady said the two children were playfellows, and she was sure you would not object."

"The lady is quite right. Mrs. Zant's illness is not serious, I hope?"

"I think not, sir. But I should like to say something in her interests. May I? Thank you." She advanced a step nearer to him, and spoke her next words in a whisper. "Take Mrs. Zant away from this place, and lose no time in doing it."

Mr. Rayburn was on his guard. He merely asked: "Why?"

The housekeeper answered in a curiously indirect manner -- partly in jest, as it seemed, and partly in earnest.

"When a man has lost his wife," she said, "there's some difference of opinion in Parliament, as I hear, whether he does right or wrong, if he marries his wife's sister. Wait a bit! I'm coming to the point. My master is one who has a long head on his shoulders; he sees consequences which escape the notice of people like me. In his way of thinking, if one man may marry his wife's sister, and no harm done, where's the objection if another man pays a *compliment* to the family, and marries his brother's widow? My master, if you please, is that other man. Take the widow away before she marries him."

Curiously -
Inquisitively
Objection -
Complaint protest
Confronted
-Opposed

This was beyond *endurance*.

"You insult Mrs. Zant," Mr. Rayburn answered, "if you suppose that such a thing is possible!"

"Oh! I insult her, do I? Listen to me. One of three things will happen. She will be *entrapped* into *consenting* to it -- or frightened into consenting to it -- or drugged into consenting to it --"

Mr. Rayburn was too *indignant* to let her go on.

"You are talking nonsense," he said. "There can be no marriage; the law forbids it."

"Are you one of the people who see no further than their noses?" she asked *insolently*. "Won't the law take his money? Is he obliged to mention that he is related to her by marriage, when he buys the license?" She paused; her humour changed; she stamped furiously on the floor. The true motive that animated her showed itself in her next words, and warned Mr. Rayburn to grant a more favourable hearing than he had *accorded* to her yet. "If you won't stop it," she burst out, "I will! If he marries anybody, he is bound to marry ME. Will you take her away? I ask you, for the last time -- will you take her away?"

The tone in which she made that final appeal to him had its effect.

"I will go back with you to John Zant's house," he said, "and judge for myself."

She laid her hand on his arm:

"I must go first -- or you may not be let in. Follow me in five minutes; and don't knock at the street door."

On the point of leaving him, she abruptly returned.

"We have forgotten something," she said. "Suppose my master refuses to see you. His temper might get the better of him; he might make it so unpleasant for you that you would be obliged to go."

"My temper might get the better of me," Mr. Rayburn replied; "and -- if I thought it was in Mrs. Zant's interests -- I might refuse to leave the house unless she *accompanied* me."

"That will never do, sir."

"Why not?"

"Because I should be the person to suffer."

"In what way?"

Entrapped -
Captured
Consenting -
Approving
Indignant - *Angry, Resentful*
Accorded - *Agreed*

"In this way. If you picked a quarrel with my master, I should be blamed for it because I showed you upstairs. Besides, think of the lady. You might frighten her out of her senses, if it came to a struggle between you two men."

The language was *exaggerated*; but there was a force in this last objection which Mr. Rayburn was obliged to acknowledge.

"And, after all," the housekeeper continued, "he has more right over her than you have. He is related to her, and you are only her friend."

Mr. Rayburn declined to let himself be influenced by this consideration, "Mr. John Zant is only related to her by marriage," he said. "If she prefers trusting in me -- come what may of it, I will be worthy of her confidence."

The housekeeper shook her head.

"That only means another quarrel," she answered. "The wise way, with a man like my master, is the peaceable way. We must manage to deceive him."

"I don't like *deceit*."

"In that case, sir, I'll wish you good-by. We will leave Mrs. Zant to do the best she can for herself." Mr. Rayburn was unreasonable. He positively refused to adopt this *alternative*.

"Will you hear what I have got to say?" the housekeeper asked.

"There can be no harm in that," he admitted. "Go on."

She took him at his word.

"When you called at our house," she began, "did you notice the doors in the passage, on the first floor? Very well. One of them is the door of the drawing-room, and the other is the door of the library. Do you remember the drawing-room, sir?"

"I thought it a large well-lighted room," Mr. Rayburn answered. "And I noticed a doorway in the wall, with a handsome curtain hanging over it."

"That's enough for our purpose," the housekeeper resumed. "On the other side of the curtain, if you had looked in, you would have found the library. Suppose my master is as polite as usual, and begs to be excused for not receiving you, because it is an *inconvenient* time. And suppose you are polite on your side and take yourself off by the drawing-room

Exaggerated - *Magnified*
Deceit - *Fraud, Trickery*
Inconvenient - *Bothersome*
Resumed - *Assumed, to begin again*

door. You will find me waiting downstairs, on the first landing. Do you see it now?"

"I can't say I do."

"You surprise me, sir. What is to prevent us from getting back softly into the library, by the door in the passage? And why shouldn't we use that second way into the library as a means of discovering what may be going on in the drawing-room? Safe behind the curtain, you will see him if he behaves *uncivilly* to Mrs. Zant, or you will hear her if she calls for help. In either case, you may be as rough and ready with my master as you find needful; it will be he who has frightened her, and not you. And who can blame the poor housekeeper because Mr. Rayburn did his duty, and protected a helpless woman? There is my plan, sir. Is it worth trying?"

He answered, sharply enough: "I don't like it."

The housekeeper opened the door again, and wished him good-by.

If Mr. Rayburn had felt no more than an ordinary interest in Mrs. Zant, he would have let the woman go. As it was, he stopped her; and, after some further protest (which proved to be useless), he ended in giving way.

"You promise to follow my directions?" she stipulated.

He gave the promise. She smiled, ***nodded***, and left him. True to his instructions, Mr. Rayburn ***reckoned*** five minutes by his watch, before he followed her.

XII

The housekeeper was waiting for him, with the street-door ajar.

"They are both in the drawing-room," she whispered, leading the way upstairs. "Step softly, and take him by surprise."

A table of oblong shape stood midway between the drawing-room walls. At the end of it which was nearest to the window, Mrs. Zant was ***pacing*** to and fro across the breadth of the room. At the opposite end of the table, John Zant was seated. Taken completely by surprise, he showed himself in his true character. He started to his feet, and protested with an oath against the ***intrusion*** which had been committed on him.

Heedless of his action and his language, Mr. Rayburn could look at nothing, could think of nothing, but Mrs. Zant. She was

Uncivilly - *Without manners, disrespectful*
Pacing - *Rate of movement heedless careless*
Intrusion - *Forceful entry*

still walking slowly to and fro, **unconscious** of the words of sympathy which he addressed to her, **insensible** even as it seemed to the presence of other persons in the room.

John Zant's voice broke the silence. His temper was under control again: he had his reasons for still remaining on friendly terms with Mr. Rayburn.

"I am sorry I forgot myself just now," he said.

Mr. Rayburn's interest was *concentrated* on Mrs. Zant; he took no notice of the *apology*.

"When did this happen?" he asked.

"About a quarter of an hour ago. I was fortunately at home. Without speaking to me, without noticing me, she walked upstairs like a person in a dream."

Mr. Rayburn suddenly pointed to Mrs. Zant.

"Look at her!" he said. "There's a change!"

All restlessness in her movements had come to an end. She was standing at the further end of the table, which was nearest to the window, in the full flow of sunlight pouring at that moment over her face. Her eyes looked out straight before her -- void of all expression. Her lips were a little parted: her head drooped slightly toward her shoulder, in an attitude which suggested listening for something or waiting for something. In the warm brilliant light, she stood before the two men, a living creature self-*isolated* in a stillness like the stillness of death.

John Zant was ready with the expression of his opinion.

"A nervous seizure," he said. "Something *resembling* catalepsy, as you see."

"Have you sent for a doctor?"

"A doctor is not wanted."

"I beg your pardon. It seems to me that medical help is absolutely necessary."

"Be so good as to remember," Mr. John Zant answered, "that the decision rests with me, as the lady's relative. I am sensible of the honour which your visit confers on me. But the time has been unhappily chosen. Forgive me if I suggest that you will do well to retire."

Mr. Rayburn had not forgotten the housekeeper's advice, or the promise which she had *exacted* from him. But the expression in John Zant's face was a serious trial to his self-control. He hesitated, and looked back at Mrs. Zant.

Concentrated - *Clustered, gathered together closely*
Apology - *Excuse, regret*
Self-isolated - *To separate oneself*
Resembling - *Similar*

If he *provoked* a quarrel by remaining in the room, the one *alternative* would be the removal of her by force. Fear of the consequences to herself, if she was suddenly and roughly roused from her trance, was the one consideration which reconciled him to **submission**. He withdrew.

The housekeeper was waiting for him below, on the first landing. When the door of the drawing-room had been closed again, she signed to him to follow her, and returned up the stairs. After another struggle with himself, he obeyed. They entered the library from the corridor -- and placed themselves behind the closed curtain which hung over the doorway. It was easy so to arrange the edge of the *drapery* as to observe, without exciting suspicion, whatever was going on in the next room.

Mrs. Zant's brother-in-law was approaching her at the time when Mr. Rayburn saw him again.

In the instant afterward, she moved -- before he had completely passed over the space between them. Her still figure began to tremble. She lifted her drooping head. For a moment there was a *shrinking* in her -- as if she had been touched by something. She seemed to recognize the touch: she was still again.

John Zant watched the change. It suggested to him that she was beginning to recover her senses. He tried the experiment of speaking to her.

"My love, my sweet angel, come to the heart that adores you!"

He advanced again; he passed into the flood of sunlight pouring over her.

"Rouse yourself!" he said.

She still remained in the same position; apparently at his mercy, neither hearing him nor seeing him.

"Rouse yourself!" he repeated. "My darling, come to me!"

At the instant when he attempted to *embrace* her -- at the instant when Mr. Rayburn rushed into the room -- John Zant's arms, suddenly turning rigid, remained outstretched. With a shriek of horror, he struggled to draw them back -- struggled, in the empty brightness of the sunshine, as if some invisible grip had seized him.

"What has got me?" the wretch screamed. "Who is holding my hands? Oh, the cold of it! the cold of it!"

Provoked - *Initiated*
Alternative - *Optional*
Drapery - *Clothing*
Shrinking - *Contracting*
Embrace - *Hug*

His features became convulsed; his eyes turned upward until only the white eyeballs were visible. He fell *prostrate* with a crash that shook the room.

The housekeeper ran in. She knelt by her master's body. With one hand she loosened his cravat. With the other she pointed to the end of the table.

Mrs. Zant still kept her place; but there was another change. Little by little, her eyes recovered their natural living expression -- then slowly closed. She *tottered* backward from the table, and lifted her hands wildly, as if to grasp at something which might support her. Mr. Rayburn hurried to her before she fell -- lifted her in his arms -- and carried her out of the room.

One of the servants met them in the hall. He sent her for a carriage. In a quarter of an hour more, Mrs. Zant was safe under his care at the hotel.

XIII

That night a note, written by the housekeeper, was delivered to Mrs. Zant.

"The doctors give little hope. The paralytic stroke is spreading upward to his face. If death spares him, he will live a helpless man. I shall take care of him to the last. As for you -- forget him."

Mrs. Zant gave the note to Mr. Rayburn.

"Read it, and destroy it," she said. "It is written in ignorance of the terrible truth."

He obeyed -- and looked at her in silence, waiting to hear more. She hid her face. The few words she had addressed to him, after a struggle with herself, fell slowly and *reluctantly* from her lips.

She said: "No mortal hand held the hands of John Zant. The *guardian* spirit was with me. The promised protection was with me. I know it. I wish to know no more."

Having spoken, she rose to retire. He opened the door for her, seeing that she needed rest in her own room.

Left by himself, he began to consider the *prospect* that was before him in the future. How was he to regard the woman who had just left him? As a poor creature weakened by disease, the victim of her own nervous *delusion*? or as the chosen object of

Prostrate - *To lay flat*
Tottered - *Staggered*
Reluctantly - *Casually*
Guardian - *Protector, defender*

Greatest Ghost Stories

a supernatural revelation -- unparalleled by any similar *revelation* that he had heard of, or had found recorded in books? His first discovery of the place that she really held in his estimation dawned on his mind, when he felt himself *recoiling* from the conclusion which presented her to his pity, and yielding to the nobler *conviction* which felt with her faith, and raised her to a place apart among other women.

XIV

They left St. Sallins the next day.

Arrived at the end of the journey, Lucy held fast by Mrs. Zant's hand. Tears were rising in the child's eyes.

"Are we to bid her good-by?" she said sadly to her father.

He seemed to be unwilling to trust himself to speak; he only said:

"My dear, ask her yourself."

But the result justified him. Lucy was happy again.

Food For Thought

What did the ghost of Mrs. Zant's husband do with his brother who had intentions to marry Mrs. Zant? Do you think the ghost would have allowed Mrs. Zant to marry Mr. Rayburn? What happened at the end of the story?

Justified - *To uphold*
Revelation - *Disclosure*
Recoiling - *To draw back*
Conviction - *A firm belief*

An Understanding

Q. 1. Who was Mr. Rayburn and Lucy? Give a brief character sketch of Mr. Rayburn.
Ans. _____
_____
_____
_____
_____

Q. 2. Who was Mrs. Zant and what had happened with her? Where did she meet Mr. Rayburn?
Ans. _____
_____
_____
_____
_____

Q. 3. What did Mrs. Zant experience in the Kensington Gardens? What was the aim of Mr. Zant's brother - in - law?
Ans. _____
_____
_____
_____
_____

Q. 4. How did Mr. Rayburn rescue Mrs. Zant? Describe the incident briefly in your own words. What did Mr. Rayburn hope to do?
Ans. _____
_____
_____
_____
_____

The Secret of Macarger's Gulch
~ Ambrose Bierce

NOrthwestwardly from Indian Hill, about nine miles as the crow flies, is Macarger's Gulch. It is not much of a gulch -- a mere *depression* between two wooded ridges of inconsiderable height. From its mouth up to its head -- for gulches, like rivers, have an anatomy of their own -- the distance does not exceed two miles, and the width at bottom is at only one place more than a dozen yards; for most of the distance on either side of the little brook which drains it in winter, and goes dry in the early spring, there is no level ground at all; the steep slopes of the hills, covered with an almost *inpenetrable* growth of *manzanita* and *chemisal*, are parted by nothing but the width of the watercourse. No one but an occasional *enterprising* hunter of the vicinity ever goes into Macarger's Gulch, and five miles away it is unknown, even by name. Within that distance in any direction are far more conspicuous *topographical* features without names, and one might try in vain to ascertain by local inquiry the origin of the name of this one.

About midway between the head and the mouth of Macarger's Gulch, the hill on the right as you ascend is cloven by another gulch, a short dry one, and at the junction of the two is a level space of two or three acres, and there a few years ago stood an old board house containing one small room. How the component parts of the house, few and simple as they were, had been assembled at that almost inaccessible point is a problem in the solution of which there would be greater satisfaction than advantage. Possibly the creek bed is a reformed road. It is certain that the gulch was at one time pretty *thoroughly* prospected by miners, who must have had some means of getting in with at least pack animals carrying tools and supplies; their profits, apparently, were not such as would have justified any considerable outlay to connect Macarger's Gulch with any centre of civilization enjoying the distinction of a sawmill. The house, however, was there, most of it. It lacked a door and a window frame, and the chimney of mud and stones had fallen into an unlovely heap, overgrown with rank weeds. Such humble furniture as there may once have been and much of the lower

Depression - *Dejcetion*
Impenetrable - *Inaccessible*
manzanita - *North Amercian strubs small trees*
Chemical - *A substance produced in a chemical process*
Enterprising - *Ambitious*
Topographical - *Relief features*
Thoroughly - *Minutely*

weather-boarding, had served as fuel in the camp fires of hunters; as had also, probably, the *kerbing* of an old well, which at the time I write of existed in the form of a rather wide but not very deep depression near by.

One afternoon in the summer of 1874, I passed up Macarger's Gulch from the narrow valley into which it opens, by following the dry bed of the brook. I was quail-shooting and had made a bag of about a dozen birds by the time I had reached the house described, of whose existence I was until then unaware. After rather carelessly *inspecting* the ruin I resumed my sport, and having fairly good success prolonged it until near sunset, when it occurred to me that I was a long way from any human *habitation* -- too far to reach one by nightfall. But in my game bag was food, and the old house would *afford* shelter, if shelter were needed on a warm and dewless night in the foothills of the Sierra Nevada, where one may sleep in comfort on the pine needles, without covering. I am fond of solitude and love the night, so my resolution to 'camp out' was soon taken, and by the time that it was dark I had made my bed of *boughs* and grasses in a corner of the room and was roasting a quail at a fire that I had kindled on the hearth. The smoke escaped out of the ruined chimney, the light *illuminated* the room with a kindly glow, and as I ate my simple meal of plain bird and drank the remains of a bottle of red wine which had served me all the afternoon in place of the water, which the region did not supply, I experienced a sense of comfort which better fare and accommodations do not always give.

Nevertheless, there was something lacking. I had a sense of comfort, but not of security. I detected myself *staring* more frequently at the open doorway and blank window than I could find warrant for doing. Outside these apertures all was black, and I was unable to repress a certain feeling of apprehension as my fancy pictured the outer world and filled it with unfriendly entities, natural and supernatural -- chief among which, in their respective classes were the *grizzly* bear, which I knew was occasionally still seen in that region, and the ghost, which I had reason to think was not. Unfortunately, our feelings do not always respect the law of probabilities, and to me that evening, the possible and the impossible were equally disquieting.

Every one who has had experience in the matter must have observed that one confronts the actual and imaginary perils of the night with far less *apprehension* in the open air than in a house

Kerbing - *Bending Curving*
Inspecting - *Examining*
Habitation - *A place of residence*
Afford - *To manage*
Boughs - *Branches*
Grizzly - *Greyish*

with an open doorway. I felt this now as I lay on my leafy couch in a corner of the room next to the chimney and permitted my fire to die out. So strong became my sense of the presence of something *malign* and menacing in the place, that I found myself almost unable to withdraw my eyes from the opening, as in the deepening darkness it became more and more *indistinct*. And when the last little flame flickered and went out I *grasped* the shotgun which I had laid at my side and actually turned the *muzzle* in the direction of the now invisible entrance, my thumb on one of the hammers, ready to cock the piece, my breath suspended, my muscles rigid and tense. But later I laid down the weapon with a sense of shame and mortification. What did I fear, and why? -- I, to whom the night had been a more familiar face than that of man –

I, in whom that element of hereditary *superstition* from which none of us is altogether free had given to solitude and darkness and silence only a more alluring interest and charm! I was unable to *comprehend* my folly, and losing in the conjecture the thing conjectured of, I fell asleep. And then I dreamed.

I was in a great city in a foreign land -- a city whose people were of my own race, with minor differences of speech and costume; yet precisely what these were I could not say; my sense of them was indistinct. The city was dominated by a great castle upon an overlooking height whose name I knew, but could not speak. I walked through many streets, some broad and straight with high, modern buildings, some narrow, gloomy, and *tortuous*, between the gables of quaint old houses whose *overhanging* stories, elaborately ornamented with carvings in wood and stone, almost met above my head.

I sought some one whom I had never seen, yet knew that I should recognise when found. My quest was not aimless and fortuitous; it had a definite method. I turned from one street into another without hesitation and threaded a *maze* of intricate passages, devoid of the fear of losing my way.

Presently I stopped before a low door in a plain stone house which might have been the dwelling of an artisan of the better sort, and without announcing myself, entered. The room, rather sparely furnished, and lighted by a single window with small diamond-shaped panes, had but two occupants: a man and a woman. They took no notice of my intrusion, a circumstance which, in the manner of dreams, appeared entirely natural. They were not conversing; they sat apart, *unoccupied* and *sullen*.

Malign - *Vilify, baneful*
Indistinct - *Not clear*
Grasped - *To seize*
Muzzle - *The mouth*
Tortuous - *Painful*
Maze - *Delusion*

The woman was young and rather stout, with fine large eyes and a certain grave beauty; my memory of her expression is *exceedingly* vivid, but in dreams one does not observe the details of faces. About her shoulders was a plaid shawl. The man was older, dark, with an evil face made more forbidding by a long scar extending from near the left temple diagonally downward into the black moustache; though in my dreams it seemed rather to haunt the face as a thing apart -- I can express it no otherwise -- than to belong to it. The moment that I found the man and woman I knew them to be husband and wife.

What followed, I remember indistinctly; all was confused and inconsistent -- made so, I think, by gleams of consciousness. It was as if two pictures, the scene of my dream, and my actual surroundings, had been blended, one *overlying* the other, until the former, gradually fading, disappeared, and I was broad awake in the deserted cabin, entirely and tranquilly conscious of my situation.

My foolish fear was gone, and opening my eyes I saw that my fire, not altogether burned out, had revived by the falling of a stick and was again lighting the room. I had probably slept only a few minutes, but my commonplace dream had somehow so strongly *impressed* me that I was no longer drowsy; and after a little while I rose, pushed the embers of my fire together, and lighting my pipe proceeded in a rather *ludicrously* methodical way to meditate upon my vision.

It would have puzzled me then to say in what respect it was worth attention. In the first moment of serious thought that I gave to the matter I recognised the city of my dream as Edinburgh, where I had never been; so if the dream was a memory it was a memory of pictures and description. The recognition somehow deeply impressed me; it was as if something in my mind insisted rebelliously against will and reason on the importance of all this. And that faculty, whatever it was, asserted also a control of my speech. 'Surely,' I said aloud, quite involuntarily, 'the MacGregors must have come here from Edinburgh.'

At the moment, neither the substance of this remark nor the fact of my making it surprised me in the least; it seemed entirely natural that I should know the name of my dreamfolk and something of their history. But the absurdity of it all soon dawned upon me: I laughed aloud, knocked the ashes from my pipe and again stretched myself upon my bed of boughs and grass, where I lay staring absently into my failing fire, with no further thought

Exceedingly - *To a very great degree*
Overlying - *To lie over*
Impressed - *To affect deeply*
Ludicrously - *Ridiculously*

of either my dream or my surroundings. Suddenly the single remaining flame *crouched* for a moment, then, springing upward, lifted itself clear of its embers and expired in air. The darkness was absolute.

At that instant -- almost, it seemed, before the gleam of the blaze had faded from my eyes --

there was a dull, dead sound, as of some heavy body falling upon the floor, which shook beneath me as I lay. I sprang to a sitting posture and groped at my side for my gun; my notion was that some wild beast had leaped in through the open window. While the *flimsy* structure was still shaking from the impact I heard the sound of blows, the *scuffling* of feet upon the floor, and then -- it seemed to come from almost within reach of my hand, the sharp shrieking of a woman in mortal agony. So horrible a cry I had never heard nor *conceived*; it utterly unnerved me; I was conscious for a moment of nothing but my own terror! Fortunately my hand now found the weapon of which it was in search, and the familiar touch somewhat restored me. I leaped to my feet, straining my eyes to pierce the darkness. The violent sounds had ceased, but more terrible than these, I heard, at what seemed long intervals, the faint *intermittent* gasping of some living, dying thing!

As my eyes grew accustomed to the dim light of the coals in the fireplace, I saw first the shapes of the door and window looking blacker than the black of the walls. Next, the distinction between wall and floor became discernible, and at last I was sensible to the form and full expanse of the floor from end to end and side to side. Nothing was visible and the silence was unbroken.

With a hand that shook a little, the other still *grasping* my gun, I restored my fire and made a critical examination of the place. There was nowhere any sign that the cabin had been entered. My own tracks were visible in the dust covering the floor, but there were no others. I relit my pipe, provided fresh fuel by ripping a thin board or two from the inside of the house -- I did not care to go into the darkness out of doors -- and passed the rest of the night smoking and thinking, and feeding my fire; not for added years of life would I have permitted that little flame to *expire* again.

Some years afterward I met in Sacramento a man named Morgan, to whom I had a note of introduction from a friend in San Francisco. Dining with him one evening at his home I observed various '*trophies*' upon the wall, indicating that he

---

Crouched - *To stoop or bend low*
Flimsy - *Weak*
Scuffling - *To move in a hurry/confusion*
Conceived - *To form a notion*
Intermittent - *Stopping or ceasing for a time*

was fond of shooting. It turned out that he was, and in relating some of his feats he mentioned having been in the region of my adventure.

'Mr. Morgan,' I asked abruptly, 'do you know a place up there called Macarger's Gulch?'

'I have good reason to,' he replied; 'it was I who gave to the newspapers, last year, the accounts of the finding of the skeleton there.'

I had not heard of it; the accounts had been published, it appeared, while I was absent in the East.

'By the way,' said Morgan, 'the name of the gulch is a *corruption*; it should have been called "MacGregor's." My dear,' he added, speaking to his wife, 'Mr. Elderson has upset his wine.'

That was hardly accurate -- I had simply dropped it, glass and all.

'There was an old *shanty* once in the gulch,' Morgan resumed when the ruin *wrought* by my awkwardness had been repaired, 'but just previously to my visit it had been blown down, or rather blown away, for its *debris* was scattered all about, the very floor being parted, plank from plank. Between two of the sleepers still in position I and my companion observed the remnant of a plaid shawl, and examining it found that it was wrapped about the shoulders of the body of a woman; of course but little remained besides the bones, partly covered with fragments of clothing, and brown dry skin. But we will spare Mrs. Morgan,' he added with a smile. The lady had indeed exhibited signs of *disgust* rather than sympathy.

'It is necessary to say, however,' he went on, 'that the skull was *fractured* in several places, as by blows of some blunt instrument; and that instrument itself -- a pick-handle, still stained with blood -- lay under the boards near by.'

Mr. Morgan turned to his wife. 'Pardon me, my dear,' he said with affected *solemnity*, 'for mentioning these disagreeable particulars, the natural though *regrettable* incidents of a conjugal quarrel -- resulting, doubtless, from the luckless wife's *insubordination*.'

'I ought to be able to overlook it,' the lady replied with *composure*; 'you have so many times asked me to in those very words.'

I thought he seemed rather glad to go on with his story.

'From these and other circumstances,' he said, 'the coroner's jury found that the deceased, Janet MacGregor, came to her death

Expire - *To die*
Corruption - *Moral perversion*
Shanty - *Crudely built hut*
Wrought - *Worked, laboured*
Debris - *the remains or trash*
Fractured - *The breaking of a bone or cartilage*

from blows *inflicted* by some person to the jury unknown; but it was added that the *evidence* pointed strongly to her husband, Thomas MacGregor, as the guilty person. But Thomas MacGregor has never been found nor heard of. It was learned that the couple came from Edinburgh, but not -- my dear, do you not observe that Mr. Elderson's bone-plate has water in it?'

I had deposited a chicken bone in my finger bowl.

'In a little cupboard I found a photograph of MacGregor, but it did not lead to his capture.'

'Will you let me see it?' I said.

The picture showed a dark man with an evil face made more *forbidding* by a long scar extending from near the temple diagonally downward into the black moustache.

'By the way, Mr. Elderson,' said my *affable* host, 'may I know why you asked about "Macarger's Gulch"?'

'I lost a mule near there once,' I replied, 'and the mischance has -- has quite -- upset me.'

'My dear,' said Mr. Morgan, with the mechanical *intonation* of an *interpreter* translating, 'the loss of Mr. Elderson's mule has peppered his coffee.'

Food For Thought

Who was the deceased and how did her husband, Thomas Macgregor kill her? Do you think that the narrator, Mr. Elderson dreamt of Janet Macgregor and her husband when he spent that night in the lonely house or was it the ghost of Ms. Janet Macgregor? How did Elderson recognise the city of his dream as Edinburgh?

Inflicted - *Afflicted*
Evidence - *Proof*
Forbidding - *Preventing*
Affable - *Cordial, friendly*
Intonation - *Changing patterns of the pitch of avoice*
Interpreter - *A person who translates orally*

An understanding

Q. 1. Where is Macgreger's Gulch? Why did the narrator, Mr. Elderson go to this place? What had he find there?
Ans. _____
_____
_____
_____
_____

Q. 2. Why was Mr. Elderson feeling uneasy and insecure in the desolate house? What happened in that house during the night? What did Elderson dream and what happened after that?
Ans. _____
_____
_____
_____
_____

Q. 3. Who was Mr. Morgan and where did Mr. Elderson meet him? What happened when he was dining with Mr. Morgan?
Ans. _____
_____
_____
_____
_____

Q. 4. "The name of the gulch is a corruption, it should have been called Macgregor's." Why did Mr. Morgan say this and what effect did it have on Mr. Elderson?
Ans. _____
_____
_____
_____
_____

The Moonlit Road
Ambrose Bierce

1. Statement of Joel Hetman, Jr.

I am the most unfortunate of men. Rich, respected, fairly well educated and of sound health -- with many other advantages usually valued by those having them and *coveted* by those who have them not -- I sometimes think that I should be less unhappy if they had been denied me, for then the contrast between my outer and my inner life would not be *continually* demanding a painful attention. In the stress of *privation* and the need of effort I might sometimes forget the sombre secret ever baffling the conjecture that it compels.

I am the only child of Joel and Julia Hetman. The one was a well-to-do country gentleman, the other a beautiful and accomplished woman to whom he was passionately attached with what I now know to have been a jealous and *exacting* devotion. The family home was a few miles from Nashville, Tennessee, a large, irregularly built dwelling of no particular order of architecture, a little way off the road, in a park of trees and shrubbery.

At the time of which I write I was nineteen years old, a student at Yale. One day I received a telegram from my father of such urgency that in compliance with its unexplained demand I left at once for home. At the railway station in Nashville a distant relative awaited me to apprise me of the reason for my recall: my mother had been barbarously murdered -- why and by whom none could *conjecture*, but the circumstances were these.

My father had gone to Nashville, intending to return the next afternoon. Something prevented his *accomplishing* the business in hand, so he returned on the same night, arriving just before the dawn. In his testimony before the coroner he explained that having no latchkey and not caring to disturb the sleeping servants, he had, with no clearly defined intention, gone round to the rear of the house. As he turned an angle of the building, he heard a sound as of a door gently closed, and saw in the darkness, *indistinctly*, the figure of a man, which instantly disappeared among the trees of the lawn. A hasty *pursuit* and brief search of the grounds in the belief that the trespasser was some one secretly visiting a servant proving

---

Coveted - *Wrongful desire*
Exacting - *Rigid or severe in demands*
Conjecture - *Guess, speculation*
Accomplishing - *Succeeding*
Pursuit - *Chase, hunt*

Greatest Ghost Stories

fruitless, he entered at the unlocked door and mounted the stairs to my mother's chamber. Its door was open, and stepping into black darkness he fell headlong over some heavy object on the floor. I may spare myself the details; it was my poor mother, dead of **strangulation** by human hands!

Nothing had been taken from the house, the servants had heard no sound, and excepting those terrible finger-marks upon the dead woman's throat -- dear God! that I might forget them! -- no trace of the *assassin* was ever found.

I gave up my studies and remained with my father, who, naturally, was greatly changed. Always of a sedate, **taciturn disposition**, he now fell into so deep a dejection that nothing could hold his attention, yet anything -- a footfall, the sudden closing of a door -- aroused in him a fitful interest; one might have called it an *apprehension*. At any small surprise of the senses he would start visibly and sometimes turn pale, then relapse into a melancholy apathy deeper than before. I suppose he was what is called a 'nervous wreck.' As to me, I was younger then than now -- there is much in that. Youth is Gilead, in which is balm for every wound. Ah, that I might again dwell in that enchanted land! Unacquainted with grief, I knew not how to appraise my *bereavement*; I could not rightly estimate the strength of the stroke.

One night, a few months after the dreadful event, my father and I walked home from the city. The full moon was about three hours above the eastern horizon; the entire countryside had the *solemn* stillness of a summer night; our footfalls and the ceaseless song of the katydids were the only sound, aloof. Black shadows of bordering trees lay athwart the road, which, in the short reaches between, gleamed a ghostly white. As we approached the gate to our dwelling, whose front was in shadow, and in which no light shone, my father suddenly stopped and *clutched* my arm, saying, hardly above his breath:

'God! God! what is that?'

'I hear nothing,' I replied.

'But see -- see!' he said, pointing along the road, directly ahead.

I said: 'Nothing is there. Come, father, let us go in -- you are ill.'

He had released my arm and was standing rigid and motionless in the centre of the *illuminated* roadway, staring like

Assassin - *Murderer*
Taciturn - *Stern*
Disposition - *Final settlement*
Apprehension - *Opinion*
Bereavement - *A period of mourning*
Illuminated - *Lighted*

one bereft of sense. His face in the moonlight showed a pallor and fixity inexpressibly *distressing*. I pulled gently at his sleeve, but he had forgotten my existence. Presently he began to retire backward, step by step, never for an instant removing his eyes from what he saw, or thought he saw. I turned half round to follow, but stood irresolute. I do not recall any feeling of fear, unless a sudden chill was its physical *manifestation*. It seemed as if an icy wind had touched my face and enfolded my body from head to foot; I could feel the stir of it in my hair.

At that moment my attention was drawn to a light that suddenly streamed from an upper window of the house: one of the servants, awakened by what mysterious *premonition* of evil who can say, and in obedience to an impulse that she was never able to name, had lit a lamp. When I turned to look for my father he was gone, and in all the years that have passed no whisper of his fate has come across the borderland of conjecture from the realm of the unknown.

2. Statement of Caspar Grattan

To-day I am said to live, to-morrow, here in this room, will lie a senseless shape of clay that all too long was I. If anyone lift the cloth from the face of that unpleasant thing it will be in *gratification* of a mere morbid curiosity. Some, doubtless, will go further and inquire, 'Who was he?' In this writing I supply the only answer that I am able to make -- Caspar Grattan. Surely, that should be enough. The name has served my small need for more than twenty years of a life of unknown length. True, I gave it to myself, but lacking another I had the right. In this world one must have a name; it prevents confusion, even when it does not establish identity. Some, though, are known by numbers, which also seem inadequate distinctions.

One day, for illustration, I was passing along a street of a city, far from here, when I met two men in uniform, one of whom, half pausing and looking curiously into my face, said to his companion, 'That man looks like 767.' Something in the number seemed familiar and horrible. Moved by an uncontrollable impulse, I sprang into a side street and ran until I fell *exhausted* in a countrylane.

I have never forgotten that number, and always it comes to memory attended by *gibbering obscenity, peals* of joyless

Distressing - *Great pain*
Manifestation - *Display*
Premonition - *Forewarning*
Gratification - *Reward*

laughter, the clang of iron doors. So I say a name, even if self-bestowed, is better than a number. In the register of the potter's field I shall soon have both. What wealth!

Of him who shall find this paper I must beg a little consideration. It is not the history of my life; the knowledge to write that is denied me. This is only a record of broken and apparently unrelated memories, some of them as distinct and sequent as brilliant beads upon a thread, others remote and strange, having the character of crimson dreams with interspaces blank and black -- witch-fires glowing still and red in a great *desolation*.

Standing upon the shore of eternity, I turn for a last look landward over the course by which I came. There are twenty years of footprints fairly distinct, the impressions of bleeding feet. They lead through poverty and pain, devious and unsure, as of one *staggering* beneath a burden -- Remote, unfriended, melancholy, slow.

Ah, the poet's prophecy of Me -- how admirable, how dreadfully admirable!

Backward beyond the beginning of this via *dolorosa* -- this epic of suffering with episodes of sin -- I see nothing clearly; it comes out of a cloud. I know that it spans only twenty years, yet I am an old man.

One does not remember one's birth -- one has to be told. But with me it was different; life came to me full-handed and dowered me with all my faculties and powers. Of a previous existence I know no more than others, for all have *stammering intimations* that may be memories and may be dreams. I know only that my first consciousness was of maturity in body and mind -- a consciousness accepted without surprise or conjecture. I merely found myself walking in a forest, half-clad, footsore, *unutterably weary* and hungry. Seeing a farmhouse, I approached and asked for food, which was given me by one who inquired my name. I did not know, yet knew that all had names. Greatly embarrassed, I retreated, and night coming on, lay down in the forest and slept.

The next day I entered a large town which I shall not name. Nor shall I recount further incidents of the life that is now to end -- a life of wandering, always and everywhere haunted by an *overmastering* sense of crime in punishment of wrong and of terror in punishment of crime. Let me see if I can reduce it to *narrative*.

Dolorosa - *The sorrowful mother of Lord Christ*
Stammering - *Hesitating voice*
Intimidations - *Fill with fear*
Weary - *Tired*

I seem once to have lived near a great city, a prosperous planter, married to a woman whom I loved and distrusted. We had, it sometimes seems, one child, a youth of brilliant parts and promise. He is at all times a vague figure, never clearly drawn, frequently altogether out of the picture.

One luckless evening it occurred to me to test my wife's fidelity in a vulgar, commonplace way familiar to everyone who has acquaintance with the literature of fact and fiction. I went to the city, telling my wife that I should be absent until the following afternoon. But I returned before *daybreak* and went to the rear of the house, purposing to enter by a door with which I had secretly so tampered that it would seem to lock, yet not actually fasten. As I approached it, I heard it gently open and close, and saw a man steal away into the darkness. With murder in my heart, I sprang after him, but he had vanished without even the bad luck of identification. Sometimes now I cannot even *persuade* myself that it was a human being.

Crazed with jealousy and rage, blind and bestial with all the elemental passions of insulted manhood, I entered the house and sprang up the stairs to the door of my wife's chamber. It was closed, but having tampered with its lock also, I easily entered, and despite the black darkness soon stood by the side of her bed. My groping hands told me that although *disarranged* it was unoccupied.

'She is below,' I thought, 'and terrified by my entrance has *evaded* me in the darkness of the hall.' With the purpose of seeking her I turned to leave the room, but took a wrong direction -- the right one! My foot struck her, cowering in a corner of the room. Instantly my hands were at her throat, stifling a shriek, my knees were upon her struggling body; and there in the darkness, without a word of accusation or reproach, I strangled her till she died! There ends the dream. I have related it in the past tense, but the present would be the fitter form, for again and again the sombre tragedy *re-enacts* itself in my consciousness -- over and over I lay the plan, I suffer the *confirmation*, I redress the wrong. Then all is blank; and afterward the rains beat against the *grimy* windowpanes, or the snows fall upon my scant attire, the wheels rattle in the *squalid* streets where my life lies in poverty and mean employment. If there is ever sunshine I do not recall it; if there are birds they do not sing.

Daybreak - *The first appearance of day light*
Persuade - *To urge, convince*
Evaded - *To escape*
Re-enacts - *To make into an act*
Grimy - *Dirty, squalid*

There is another dream, another vision of the night. I stand among the shadows in a moonlit road. I am aware of another presence, but whose I cannot rightly determine. In the shadow of a great dwelling I catch the gleam of white garments; then the figure of a woman confronts me in the road -- my murdered wife! There is death in the face; there are marks upon the throat. The eyes are fixed on mine with an infinite gravity which is not reproach, nor hate, nor menace, nor anything less terrible than recognition. Before this awful apparition I retreat in terror -- a terror that is upon me as I write. I can no longer rightly shape the words. See! they -- Now I am calm, but truly there is no more to tell: the incident ends where it began -- in darkness and in doubt.

Yes, I am again in control of myself: 'the captain of my soul.' But that is not respite; it is another stage and phase of *expiation*. My penance, constant in degree, is mutable in kind: one of its variants is *tranquillity*. After all, it is only a life-sentence. 'To Hell for life' -- that is a foolish penalty: the culprit chooses the duration of his punishment. To-day my term *expires*.

To each and all, the peace that was not mine.

3. Statement of the Late Julia Hetman, through the Medium Bayrolles

I had retired early and fallen almost immediately into a peaceful sleep, from which I awoke with that indefinable sense of peril which is, I think, a common experience in that other, earlier life. Of its unmeaning character, too, I was entirely persuaded, yet that did not banish it. My husband, Joel Hetman, was away from home; the servants slept in another part of the house. But these were familiar conditions; they had never before distressed me. Nevertheless, the strange terror grew so insupportable that conquering my *reluctance* to move I sat up and lit the lamp at my bedside. Contrary to my expectation this gave me no relief; the light seemed rather an added danger, for I reflected that it would shine out under the door, ***disclosing*** my presence to whatever evil thing might lurk outside. You that are still in the flesh, subject to horrors of the imagination, think what a monstrous fear that must be which seeks in darkness security from malevolent existences of the night. That is to spring to close quarters with an unseen enemy -- the strategy of despair!

Extinguishing the lamp I pulled the bedclothing about my head and lay trembling and silent, unable to shriek, forgetful to

Squalid - *Foul and repulsive*
Expiation - *Faithful, loyal*
Tranquillity - *Calm, quietude*
Expires - *To come to an end, terminate*
Reluctance - *Unwillingness*

pray. In this *pitiable* state I must have lain for what you call hours -- with us there are no hours, there is no time.

At last it came -- a soft, irregular sound of footfalls on the stairs! They were slow, hesitant, uncertain, as of something that did not see its way; to my disordered reason all the more terrifying for that, as the approach of some blind and mindless malevolence to which is no appeal. I even thought that I must have left the hall lamp burning and the groping of this creature proved it a monster of the night. This was foolish and inconsistent with my previous dread of the light, but what would you have? Fear has no brains; it is an idiot. The *dismal* witness that it bears and the cowardly counsel that it whispers are unrelated. We know this well, we who have passed into the Realm of Terror, who skulk in eternal dusk among the scenes of our former lives, invisible even to ourselves, and one another, yet hiding forlorn in lonely places; yearning for speech with our loved ones, yet dumb, and as fearful of them as they of us. Sometimes the disability is removed, the law suspended: by the deathless power of love or hate we break the spell -- we are seen by those whom we would warn, *console*, or punish. What form we seem to them to bear we know not; we know only that we terrify even those whom we most wish to comfort, and from whom we most crave tenderness and sympathy.

Forgive, I pray you, this *inconsequent digression* by what was once a woman. You who consult us in this imperfect way -- you do not understand. You ask foolish questions about things unknown and things *forbidden*. Much that we know and could impart in our speech is meaningless in yours. We must communicate with you through a stammering intelligence in that small fraction of our language that you yourselves can speak. You think that we are of another world. No, we have knowledge of no world but yours, though for us it holds no sunlight, no warmth, no music, no laughter, no song of birds, nor any *companionship*. O God! what a thing it is to be a ghost, cowering and shivering in an altered world, a prey to *apprehension* and despair!

No, I did not die of fright: the Thing turned and went away. I heard it go down the stairs, hurriedly, I thought, as if itself in sudden fear. Then I rose to call for help. Hardly had my shaking hand found the door-knob when -- merciful heaven! -- I heard it returning. Its footfalls as it remounted the stairs were rapid, heavy and loud; they shook the house. I fled to an angle of the

Disclosing - *Reveal*
Extinguishing - *To put out a fire, light, etc.*
Dismal - *Gloomy*
Console - *Solace*
Digression - *Deviation*
Forbidden - *Prohibited*

wall and crouched upon the floor. I tried to pray. I tried to call the name of my dear husband. Then I heard the door thrown open. There was an interval of unconsciousness, and when I revived I felt a strangling clutch upon my throat -- felt my arms *feebly* beating against something that bore me backward -- felt my tongue *thrusting* itself from between my teeth! And then I passed into this life.

No, I have no knowledge of what it was. The sum of what we knew at death is the measure of what we know afterward of all that went before. Of this existence we know many things, but no new light falls upon any page of that; in memory is written all of it that we can read. Here are no heights of truth overlooking the confused landscape of that dubitable domain. We still dwell in the Valley of the Shadow, **lurk** in its desolate places, peering from brambles and thickets at its mad, malign inhabitants. How should we have new knowledge of that fading past?

What I am about to relate happened on a night. We know when it is night, for then you retire to your houses and we can venture from our places of **concealment** to move unafraid about our old homes, to look in at the windows, even to enter and gaze upon your faces as you sleep. I had lingered long near the dwelling where I had been so cruelly changed to what I am, as we do while any that we love or hate remain. Vainly I had sought some method of *manifestation*, some way to make my continued existence and my great love and poignant pity understood by my husband and son. Always if they slept they would wake, or if in my desperation I dared approach them when they were awake, would turn toward me the terrible eyes of the living, frightening me by the glances that I sought from the purpose that I held.

On this night I had searched for them without success, fearing to find them; they were nowhere in the house, nor about the moonlit dawn. For, although the sun is lost to us for ever, the moon, full-orbed or slender, remains to us. Sometimes it shines by night, sometimes by day, but always it rises and sets, as in that other life.

I left the lawn and moved in the white light and silence along the road, aimless and sorrowing. Suddenly I heard the voice of my poor husband in *exclamations* of astonishment, with that of my son in reassurance and dissuasion; and there by the shadow of a group of trees they stood -- near, so near! Their faces were toward me, the eyes of the elder man fixed upon mine. He saw me

Feebly - *Physically weak*
Thrusting - *Enforcing*
Lurk - *To wait or hid secretly*
Concealment - *To keep secret*
Manifestation - *Displaying*

-- at last, at last, he saw me! In the consciousness of that, my terror fled as a cruel dream. The death-spell was broken: Love had conquered Law! Mad with *exultation* I shouted -- I must have shouted,' He sees, he sees: he will understand!' Then, controlling myself, I moved forward, smiling and consciously beautiful, to offer myself to his arms, to comfort him with *endearments*, and, with my son's hand in mine, to speak words that should restore the broken bonds between the living and the dead.

Alas! alas! his face went white with fear, his eyes were as those of a hunted animal. He backed away from me, as I advanced, and at last turned and fled into the wood -- *whither*, it is not given to me to know.

To my poor boy, left doubly desolate, I have never been able to impart a sense of my presence. Soon he, too, must pass to this Life Invisible and be lost to me for ever.

Food For Thought

Julia Hetman's husband suspected his wife of infidelity. Do you think that this was the main reason for him to kill her, or do you think that her lover killed her? Why did Julia's husband disappear into the moonlit night when he heard strange noises while walking with his son?

Impart - *Disclose, relate*
Desolate - *Deprived, solitary*
Exultation - *Triumphant joy*
Endearments - *Affectionate utterance*
Whither - *Where*

An Understanding

Q. 1. Who is the author of the story and how does the author relate the tale of the murder of Julia Hetman from three perspectives?
Ans. _____
_____
_____
_____
_____

Q. 2. What does Joel Hetman, Jr., the son of the deceased (Julia Hetman) claim?
Ans. _____
_____
_____
_____
_____

Q. 3. How did Julia Hetman relate her story of murder? Do you think that the creature, who had hidden his face was none other than her husband?
Ans. _____
_____
_____
_____
_____

Q. 4. What did Julia Hetman's husband claim? Do you think he spoke the truth? Who, according to you strangled Julia to death and why?
Ans. _____
_____
_____
_____
_____

The Haunted Valley
~Ambrose Bierce

I. How Trees Are Felled in China

A half-mile north from Jo. Dunfer's, on the road from Hutton's to Mexican Hill, the highway dips into a sunless ravine which opens out on either hand in a half-*confidential* manner, as if it had a secret to impart at some more convenient season. I never used to ride through it without looking first to the one side and then to the other, to see if the time had arrived for the *revelation*. If I saw nothing -- and I never did see anything -- there was no feeling of disappointment, for I knew the disclosure was merely withheld temporarily for some good reason which I had no right to question. That I should one day be taken into full confidence I no more doubted than I doubted the existence of Jo. Dunfer himself, through whose premises the *ravine* ran.

It was said that Jo. had once undertaken to erect a cabin in some remote part of it, but for some reason had abandoned the enterprise and constructed his present *hermaphrodite* habitation, half residence and half groggery, at the roadside, upon an extreme corner of his estate; as far away as possible, as if on purpose to show how radically he had changed his mind.

This Jo. Dunfer -- or, as he was familiarly known in the neighbourhood, Whisky Jo. -- was a very important personage in those parts. He was apparently about forty years of age, a long, shock-headed fellow, with a corded face, a gnarled arm and a knotty hand like a bunch of prison-keys. He was a hairy man, with a stoop in his walk, like that of one who is about to spring upon something and rend it.

Next to the peculiarity to which he owed his local appellation, Mr. Dunfer's most obvious characteristic was a deep-seated antipathy to the Chinese. I saw him once in a *towering* rage because one of his herdsmen had permitted a travel-heated Asian to slake his thirst at the horse-trough in front of the saloon end of Jo.'s establishment. I *ventured* faintly to *remonstrate* with Jo. for his unchristian spirit, but he merely explained that there was nothing about Chinamen in the New Testament, and strode away to wreak his displeasure

Confidential - *Private*
Revelation - *Disclosure*
Ravine - *A deep narrow steep sided valley*
hermaphrodite *- Combining two opposite qualities*
Remonstrate - *To plead in protest*

upon his dog, which also, I suppose, the inspired scribes had overlooked.

Some days afterward, finding him sitting alone in his bar-room, I **cautiously** approached the subject, when, greatly to my relief, the habitual austerity of his expression visibly softened into something that I took for condescension.

'You young Easterners,' he said, 'are a mile-and-a-half too good for this country, and you don't catch on to our play. People who don't know a Chileno from a Kanaka can afford to hang out liberal ideas about Chinese *immigration*, but a fellow that has to fight for his bone with a lot of mongrel coolies hasn't any time for foolishness.'

This long consumer, who had probably never done an honest day's work in his life, sprung the lid of a Chinese tobacco-box and with thumb and forefinger forked out a wad like a small haycock. Holding this *reinforcement* within supporting distance he fired away with renewed confidence.

'They're a flight of devouring locusts, and they're going for everything green in this God blest land, if you want to know.'

Here he pushed his reserve into the breach and when his gabble-gear was again *disengaged* resumed his uplifting discourse.

'I had one of them on this ranch five years ago, and I'll tell you about it, so that you can see the *nub* of this whole question. I didn't pan out particularly well those days -- drank more whisky than was prescribed for me and didn't seem to care for my duty as a patriotic American citizen; so I took that pagan in, as a kind of cook. But when I got religion over at the Hill and they talked of running me for the Legislature it was given to me to see the light. But what was I to do? If I gave him the go somebody else would take him, and mightn't treat him white. What was I to do? What would any good Christian do, especially one new to the trade and full to the neck with the brotherhood of Man and the fatherhood of God?'

Jo. paused for a reply, with an expression of *unstable* satisfaction, as of one who has solved a problem by a *distrusted* method. Presently he rose and swallowed a glass of whisky from a full bottle on the counter, then *resumed* his story.

'Besides, he didn't count for much -- didn't know anything and gave himself airs. They all do that. I said him nay, but he *muled* it through on that line while he lasted; but after

Cautiously - *Carefully*
Immigration - *The movement of non-active people into a country to settle*
Reinforcement - *To give added strength or support*
Nub - *A knob*
Resumed - *To begin again*
Muled - *To use roughly*

turning the other cheek seventy and seven times I doctored the dice so that he didn't last for ever. And I'm almighty glad I had the sand to do it.'

Jo.'s gladness, which somehow did not impress me, was duly and ***ostentatiously*** celebrated at the bottle.

'About five years ago I started in to stick up a shack. That was before this one was built, and I put it in another place. I set Ah Wee and a little ***cuss*** named Gopher to cutting the timber. Of course I didn't expect Ah Wee to help much, for he had a face like a day in June and big black eyes -- I guess maybe they were the damn'dest eyes in this neck o' woods.'

While delivering this trenchant thrust at common sense Mr. Dunfer absently regarded a knot-hole in the thin board partition separating the bar from the living-room, as if that were one of the eyes whose size and colour had incapacitated his servant for good service.

'Now you Eastern galoots won't believe anything against the yellow devils,' he suddenly flamed out with an appearance of ***earnestness*** not altogether convincing, 'but I tell you that Chink was the perversest scoundrel outside San Francisco. The miserable pig-tail Mongolian went to hewing away at the ***saplings*** all round the stems, like a worm o' the dust gnawing a radish. I pointed out his error as patiently as I knew how, and showed him how to cut them on two sides, so as to make them fall right; but no sooner would I turn my back on him, like this' -- and he turned it on me, ***amplifying*** the illustration by taking some more liquor -- 'than he was at it again. It was just this way: while I looked at him so' -- regarding me rather ***unsteadily*** and with evident complexity of vision -- ' he was all right; but when I looked away, so' -- taking a long pull at the bottle -- 'he defied me. Then I'd gaze at him reproachfully, so, and butter wouldn't have melted in his mouth.'

Doubtless Mr. Dunfer honestly intended the look that he fixed upon me to be merely ***reproachful***, but it was singularly fit to arouse the gravest apprehension in any unarmed person incurring it; and as I had lost all interest in his pointless and interminable narrative, I rose to go. Before I had fairly risen, he had again turned to the counter, and with a barely audible 'so,' had emptied the bottle at a gulp.

Heavens! what a yell! It was like a Titan in his last, strong agony. Jo. staggered back after emitting it, as a cannon ***recoils***

Ostentatiously - *Showy, pretentious*
Cuss - *Cusse, swear*
Earnestness - *Truthfulness, sincerity*
Saplings - *Young trees*
Amplifying - *To make larger or greater*
Reproachful - *Disgraceful*
Recoils - *To draw back, shrink*

from its own thunder, and then dropped into his chair, as if he had been 'knocked in the head' like a beef -- his eyes drawn sidewise toward the wall, with a stare of terror. Looking in the same direction, I saw that the *knothole* in the wall had indeed become a human eye -- a full, black eye, that glared into my own with an entire lack of expression more awful than the most devilish glitter. I think I must have covered my face with my hands to shut out the horrible illusion, if such it was, and Jo.'s little white man-of-all-work coming into the room broke the spell, and I walked out of the house with a sort of dazed fear that delirium tremens might be *infectious*. My horse was hitched at the watering-trough, and untying him I mounted and gave him his head, too much troubled in mind to note whither he took me.

I did not know what to think of all this, and like everyone who does not know what to think I thought a great deal, and to little purpose. The only reflection that seemed at all satisfactory was, that on the morrow I should be some miles away, with a strong *probability* of never returning. A sudden coolness brought me out of my abstraction, and looking up I found myself entering the deep shadows of the ravine. The day was stifling; and this *transition* from the pitiless, visible heat of the parched fields to the cool gloom, heavy with pungency of cedars and vocal with twittering of the birds that had been driven to its leafy asylum, was exquisitely refreshing. I looked for my mystery, as usual, but not finding the ravine in a communicative mood, *dismounted*, led my sweating animal into the undergrowth, tied him securely to a tree and sat down upon a rock to meditate.

I began bravely by analysing my pet superstition about the place. Having resolved it into its constituent elements I arranged them in convenient troops and squadrons, and collecting all the forces of my logic bore down upon them from *impregnable* premises with the thunder of irresistible conclusions and a great noise of chariots and general intellectual shouting. Then, when my big mental guns had overturned all opposition, and were growing almost inaudibly away on the horizon of pure *speculation*, the routed enemy *straggled* in upon their rear, massed silently into a solid *phalanx*, and captured me, bag and baggage. An indefinable dread came upon me. I rose to shake it off, and began threading the narrow dell by an old, grass-grown cow-path

Knothole - *A hole in a board*
Transition - *Change*
Dismounted - *To get off, alight*
Impregnable - *Invulnerable*
Straggled - *To wander*
Phalanx - *Any body of troops*

that seemed to flow along the bottom, as a substitute for the brook that Nature had neglected to provide.

The trees among which the path *straggled* were ordinary, well-behaved plants, a trifle perverted as to trunk and eccentric as to bough, but with nothing unearthly in their general aspect. A few loose boulders, which had detached themselves from the sides of the depression to set up an independent existence at the bottom, had dammed up the pathway, here and there, but their stony repose had nothing in it of the stillness of death. There was a kind of death-chamber hush in the valley, it is true, and a mysterious whisper above: the wind was just fingering the tops of the trees -- that was all.

I had not thought of connecting Jo. Dunfer's drunken narrative with what I now sought, and only when I came into a clear space and stumbled over the level trunks of some small trees did I have the revelation. This was the site of the abandoned 'shack.' The discovery was verified by noting that some of the rotting stumps were hacked all round, in a most unwoodman-like way, while others were cut straight across, and the butt ends of the corresponding trunks had the blunt wedge-form given by the axe of a master.

The opening among the trees was not more than thirty paces across. At one side was a little knoll-a natural *hillock*, bare of *shrubbery* but covered with wild grass, and on this, standing out of the grass, the *headstone* of a grave!

I do not remember that I felt anything like surprise at this discovery. I viewed that lonely grave with something of the feeling that Columbus must have had when he saw the hills and headlands of the new world. Before approaching it I leisurely completed my survey of the surroundings. I was even guilty of the affectation of winding my watch at that unusual hour, and with needless care and *deliberation*. Then I approached my mystery.

The grave -- a rather short one -- was in somewhat better repair than was consistent with its obvious age and isolation, and my eyes, I dare say, widened a trifle at a clump of unmistakable garden flowers showing evidence of recent watering. The stone had clearly enough done duty once as a doorstep. In its front was carved, or rather dug, an *inscription*. It read thus:

AH WEE -- CHINAMAN.

Age unknown. Worked for Jo. Dunfer.

Hillock - *A small hill*
Shrubbery - *A planting of shrubs*
Headstone - *A memorial stone*
Deliberation - *Careful consideration*
Inscription - *Words engraved on rock, metal*

This monument is erected by him to keep the Chink's memory green. Likewise as a warning to *Celestials* not to take on airs. Devil take 'em! She Was a Good Egg.

I cannot adequately relate my astonishment at this uncommon inscription! The meagre but sufficient identification of the deceased; the *impudent candour* of *confession*; the brutal anathema; the ludicrous change of sex and sentiment -- all marked this record as the work of one who must have been at least as much demented as bereaved. I felt that any further disclosure would be a paltry *anti-climax*, and with an unconscious regard for dramatic effect turned squarely about and walked away. Nor did I return to that part of the county for four years.

II. Who Drives Sane Oxen Should Himself be Sane

'Gee-up, there, old Fuddy-Duddy!'

This unique adjuration came from the lips of a queer little man perched upon a wagonful of firewood, behind a brace of oxen that were hauling it easily along with a simulation of mighty effort which had evidently not *imposed* on their lord and master. As that gentleman happened at the moment to be staring me squarely in the face as I stood by the roadside it was not altogether clear whether he was addressing me or his beasts; nor could I say if they were named Fuddy and Duddy and were both subjects of the *imperative* mood 'to gee-up.' Anyhow the command produced no effect on us, and the queer little man removed his eyes from mine long enough to spear Fuddy and Duddy alternately with a long pole, remarking, quietly but with feeling: 'Dern your skin,' as if they enjoyed that *integument* in common. Observing that my request for a ride took no attention, and finding myself falling slowly *astern*, I placed one foot upon the inner circumference of a hind wheel and was slowly elevated to the level of the hub, whence I boarded the concern, sans ceremonie, and scrambling forward seated myself beside the driver -- who took no notice of me until he had administered another indiscriminate castigation to his cattle, accompanied with the advice to 'buckle down, you derned Incapable!' Then, the master of the outfit (or rather the former master, for I could not suppress a *whimsical* feeling that the entire establishment was my lawful prize) trained his big, black eyes upon me with an expression strangely, and somewhat unpleasantly, familiar,

Astern - *In a backward direction*
Whimsical - *Unpredictable*
Celestials - *Heavenly*
Impudent - *Insulting, rude*
Candour - *The state of being frank*
Imperative - *Absolutely necessary*

laid down his rod -- which neither blossomed nor turned into a serpent, as I half expected -- folded his arms, and gravely demanded, 'W'at did you do to W'isky?'

My natural reply would have been that I drank it, but there was something about the query that suggested a hidden significance, and something about the man that did not invite a shallow *jest*. And so, having no other answer ready, I merely held my tongue, but felt as if I were resting under an imputation of guilt, and that my silence was being *construed* into a confession.

Just then a cold shadow fell upon my cheek, and caused me to look up. We were descending into my ravine! I cannot describe the sensation that came upon me: I had not seen it since it *unbosomed* itself four years before, and now I felt like one to whom a friend has made some sorrowing confession of crime long past, and who has basely deserted him in *consequence*. The old memories of Jo. Dunfer, his fragmentary revelation, and the unsatisfying explanatory note by the headstone, came back with singular *distinctness*. I wondered what had become of Jo., and -- I turned sharply around and asked my prisoner. He was intently watching his cattle, and without withdrawing his eyes replied:

'Gee-up, old Terrapin! He lies aside of Ah Wee up the gulch. Like to see it? They always come back to the spot -- I've been expectin' you. H-woa!'

At the enunciation of the aspirate, Fuddy-Duddy, the incapable *terrapin*, came to a dead halt, and before the vowel had died away up the ravine had folded up all his eight legs and lain down in the dusty road, regardless of the effect upon his derned skin. The queer little man slid off his seat to the ground and started up the dell without deigning to look back to see if I was following. But I was.

It was about the same season of the year, and at near the same hour of the day, of my last visit. The jays clamoured loudly, and the trees whispered darkly, as before; and I somehow traced in the two sounds a fanciful *analogy* to the open *boastfulness* of Mr. Jo. Dunfer's mouth and the mysterious reticence of his manner, and to the mingled *hardihood* and tenderness of his sole literary production -- the epitaph. All things in the valley seemed unchanged, excepting the cowpath, which was almost wholly overgrown with weeds. When

Jest - *A witty remark*
Construed - *Explain, interpret*
Terrapin - *Water tortoise*
Boastfulness - *Pride*
Analogy - *Similarity*

we came out into the 'clearing,' however, there was change enough. Among the stumps and trunks of the fallen saplings, those that had been hacked 'China fashion' were no longer distinguishable from those that were cut "Melican way.' It was as if the Old-World barbarism and the New-World civilization had reconciled their differences by the arbitration of an impartial decay -- as is the way of civilizations. The *knoll* was there, but the Hunnish brambles had overrun and all but obliterated its effete grasses; and the patrician garden-violet had capitulated to his plebeian brother -- perhaps had merely *reverted* to his original type. Another grave -- a long, robust mound -- had been made beside the first, which seemed to shrink from the comparison; and in the shadow of a new headstone the old one lay prostrate, with its marvellous inscription illegible by accumulation of leaves and soil. In point of literary merit the new was inferior to the old -- was even repulsive in its terse and s*avage jocularity*:

JO. DUNFER. DONE FOR

I turned from it with indifference, and brushing away the leaves from the tablet of the dead pagan restored to light the *mocking* words which, fresh from their long neglect, seemed to have a certain pathos. My guide, too, appeared to take on an added seriousness as he read it, and I fancied that I could detect beneath his whimsical manner something of *manliness*, almost of dignity. But while I looked at him his former aspect, so subtly unhuman, so *tantalizingly* familiar, crept back into his big eyes, repellent and attractive. I resolved to make an end of the mystery if possible.

'My friend,' I said, pointing to the smaller grave, 'did Jo. Dunfer murder that Chinaman?'

He was *leaning* against a tree and looking across the open space into the top of another, or into the blue sky beyond. He neither withdrew his eyes, nor altered his posture as he slowly replied:

'No, sir; he *justifiably homicided* him.'

'Then he really did kill him.'

'Kill 'im? I should say he did, rather. Doesn't everybody know that? Didn't he stan' up before the coroner's jury and confess it? And didn't they find a verdict of "Came to 'is death by a *wholesome* Christian sentiment workin' in the Caucasian

Knoll - *A small rounded hill*
Revered - *Respected*
Savage - *Wild*
Jocularity - *Humorously*
Tantalizing - *Provoking*

breast"? An' didn't the church at the Hill turn W'isky down for it? And didn't the *sovereign* people elect him Justice of the Peace to get even on the *gospellers*? I don't know where you were brought up.'

'But did Jo. do that because the Chinaman did not, or would not, learn to cut down trees like a white man? '

'Sure! -- it stan's so on the record, which makes it true an' legal. My knowin' better doesn't make any difference with legal truth; it wasn't my funeral and I wasn't invited to deliver an *oration*. But the fact is, W'isky was jealous o' me' -- and the little wretch actually swelled out like a turkeycock and made a pretence of adjusting an imaginary neck-tie, noting the effect in the palm of his hand, held up before him to represent a mirror.

'Jealous of you!' I repeated with ill-mannered astonishment.

'That's what I said. Why not? -- don't I look all right?'

He assumed a mocking attitude of studied grace, and *twitched* the wrinkles out of his threadbare waistcoat. Then, suddenly dropping his voice to a low pitch of singular sweetness, he continued:

'W'isky thought a lot o' that Chink; nobody but me knew how 'e doted on 'im. Couldn't bear 'im out of 'is sight, the derned protoplasm! And w'en 'e came down to this clearin' one day an' found 'im an' me neglectin' our work -- 'im asleep an' me grapplin' a *tarantula* out of 'is sleeve -- W'isky laid hold of my axe and let us have it, good an' hard! I dodged just then, for the spider bit me, but Ah Wee got it bad in the side an' tumbled about like anything. W'isky was just weighin' me out one w'en 'e saw the spider fastened on my finger; then 'e knew 'e'd make a jackass of 'imself. 'E threw away the axe and got down on 'is knees alongside of Ah Wee, who gave a last little kick and opened 'is eyes -- 'e had eyes like mine -- an' puttin' up 'is hands drew down W'isky's ugly head and held it there w'ile 'e stayed. That wasn't long, for a tremblin' ran through 'im and 'e gave a bit of a moan an' beat the game.'

During the progress of the story the narrator had become *transfigured*. The comic, or rather, the sardonic element was all out of him, and as he painted that strange scene it was with difficulty that I kept my composure. And this *consummate* actor had somehow so managed me that the sympathy due to his dramatis personae was given to himself. I stepped forward

Sovereign - *Supreme*
Gspellers - *A preacher of the Christian gospel*
Tarantula- *Larger hairy tropical spiders*
Transfigured - *Transformed*
Consummate - *Fulfill*

to grasp his hand, when suddenly a broad ***grin*** danced across his face and with a light, mocking laugh he continued:

'W'en W'isky got 'is nut out o' that 'e was a sight to see! All 'is fine clothes -- 'e dressed mighty blindin' those days -- were spoiled everlastin'! 'Is hair was tousled and 'is face -- what I could see of it -- was whiter than the ace of lilies. 'E stared once at me, and looked away as if I didn't count; an' then there were shootin' pains chasin' one another from my bitten finger into my head, and it was Gopher to the dark. That's why I wasn't at the inquest.'

'But why did you hold your tongue afterward?' I asked.

'It's that kind of tongue,' he replied, and not another word would he say about it.

'After that W'isky took to drinkin' harder an' harder, and was rabider an' rabider anti-coolie, but I don't think 'e was ever particularly glad that 'e ***dispelled*** Ah Wee. 'E didn't put on so much dog about it w'en we were alone as w'en 'e had the ear of a derned Spectacular ***Extravaganza*** like you. 'E put up that headstone and gouged the inscription accordin' to 'is varyin' moods. It took 'im three weeks, workin' between drinks. I gouged 'is in one day.

'When did Jo. die?' I asked rather absently. The answer took my breath:

'Pretty soon after I looked at 'im through that knot-hole, w'en you had put something in 'is w'isky, you derned Borgia!'

Recovering somewhat from my surprise at this ***astounding*** charge, I was half-minded to ***throttle*** the audacious accuser, but was restrained by a sudden ***conviction*** that came to me in the light of a revelation. I fixed a grave look upon him and asked, as calmly as I could: 'And when did you go loony?'

'Nine years ago!' he ***shrieked***, throwing out his clenched hands -- 'nine years ago, w'en that big brute killed the woman who loved him better than she did me! -- me who had followed 'er from San Francisco, where 'e won 'er at draw poker! -- me who had watched over 'er for years w'en the scoundrel she belonged to was ashamed to acknowledge 'er and treat 'er white! -- me who for her sake kept 'is cussed secret till it ate 'im up! -- me who w'en you poisoned the beast fulfilled 'is last request to lay 'im ***alongside*** 'er and give 'im a stone to the head of 'im! And I've never since seen 'er grave till now, for I didn't want to meet 'im here.'

Grin - *A broad smile*
Dispelled - *Alleviate, vanish*
Extravaganza - *Lavish show*
Astounding - *Overwhelming*
Throttle - *To choke suffocate*

'Meet him? Why, Gopher, my poor fellow, he is dead!'

'That's why I'm afraid of 'im.'

I followed the little wretch back to his wagon and **wrung** his hand at parting. It was now nightfall, and as I stood there at the roadside in the deepening **gloom**, watching the blank outlines of the **receding** wagon, a sound was borne to me on the evening wind -- a sound as of a series of **vigorous** thumps -- and a voice came out of the night:

'Gee-up, there, you derned old Geranium.'

Food For Thought

Wrung - *To twist forcibly*
Gloom - *Sadness, melancholy*
Receding - *Retreating*
Vigorous - *Energetic, forceful*

What had happened nine years ago? How did Jo. Dunfer kill the woman, whom Goher loved? Did Gopher kill Jo Dunfer? Why do you think that the author named the story as "The Haunted Valley"?

An Understanding

Q. 1. Who was Jo Dunfer and why was he a very important person in those parts of China? Give a brief character sketch of Mr. Dunfer and why did he have a deep - seated antipathy towards the chinese?
Ans. _____
_____
_____
_____
_____

Q. 2. Whom did the narrator give the task of cutting the timber? Why didn't he expect much from Ah Wee? Why do you think Jo Dunfer drank a lot and what was the narrator doing in that area?
Ans. _____
_____
_____
_____
_____

Q. 3. How were the relations of the white men with chinese during the time when Bierce wrote this story? Why were trees felled a lot in China at that time? How did Jo Dunfer die?
Ans. _____
_____
_____
_____
_____

Q. 4. How and Why did Joe Dunfer murder the Chinaman?
Ans. _____
_____
_____
_____
_____

The Death of Halpin Frayser
~ Ambrose Bierce

For by death is wrought greater change than hath been shown. Whereas in general the spirit that removed cometh back upon occasion, and is sometimes seen of those in flesh (appearing in the form of the body it bore) yet it hath happened that the *veritable* body without the spirit hath walked. And it is attested of those encountering who have lived to speak thereon that a lich so raised up hath no natural affection, nor remembrance thereof, but only hate. Also, it is known that some spirits which in life were benign become by death evil altogether. -- HALL.

One dark night in midsummer a man waking from a dreamless sleep in a forest lifted his head from the earth, and staring a few moments into the blackness, said: 'Catharine Larue.' He said nothing more; no reason was known to him why he should have said so much.

The man was Halpin Frayser. He lived in St. Helena, but where he lives now is uncertain, for he is dead. One who practises sleeping in the woods with nothing under him but the dry leaves and the damp earth, and nothing over him but the branches from which the leaves have fallen and the sky from which the earth has fallen, cannot hope for great longevity, and Frayser had already attained the age of thirty-two. There are persons in this world, millions of persons, and far and away the best persons, who regard that as a very advanced age. They are the children. To those who view the voyage of life from the port of departure the bark that has accomplished any considerable distance appears already in close approach to the farther shore. However, it is not certain that Halpin Frayser came to his death by *exposure*.

He had been all day in the hills west of the Napa Valley, looking for doves and such small game as was in season. Late in the afternoon it had come on to be cloudy, and he had lost his ***bearings***; and although he had only to go always downhill -- everywhere the way to safety when one is lost -- the absence of trails had so ***impeded*** him that he was overtaken by night while still in the forest. Unable in the darkness to penetrate the ***thickets*** of manzanita and other undergrowth, ***utterly***

Veritable - *Being truly*
Exposure - *Disclosure*
Bearings - *The manner in which one conducts oneself*
Impeded - *Obstructed*
Thickets - *Dense growth of shrubs, bushes*

bewildered and overcome with *fatigue*, he had lain down near the root of a large madrono and fallen into a dreamless sleep. It was hours later, in the very middle of the night, that one of God's *mysterious* messengers, gliding ahead of the incalculable host of his companions sweeping westward with the dawn line, pronounced the awakening word in the ear of the sleeper, who sat *upright* and spoke, he knew not why, a name, he knew not whose.

Halpin Frayser was not much of a philosopher, nor a scientist. The circumstance that, waking from a deep sleep at night in the midst of a forest, he had spoken aloud a name that he had not in memory and hardly had in mind did not arouse an enlightened curiosity to investigate the phenomenon. He thought it odd, and with a little *perfunctory* shiver, as if in deference to a seasonal presumption that the night was chill, he lay down again and went to sleep. But his sleep was no longer dreamless.

He thought he was walking along a dusty road that showed white in the gathering darkness of a summer night. *Whence* and whither it led, and why he travelled it, he did not know, though all seemed simple and natural, as is the way in dreams; for in the Land Beyond the Bed surprises cease from troubling and the judgment is at rest. Soon he came to a parting of the ways; leading from the highway was a road less travelled, having the appearance, indeed, of having been long abandoned, because, he thought, it led to something evil; yet he turned into it without hesitation, impelled by some imperious necessity.

As he pressed forward he became conscious that his way was haunted by invisible existences whom he could not definitely figure to his mind. From among the trees on either side he caught broken and incoherent whispers in a strange tongue which yet he partly understood. They seemed to him fragmentary utterances of a monstrous *conspiracy* against his body and soul.

It was now long after nightfall, yet the interminable forest through which he journeyed was lit with a wan glimmer having no point of *diffusion,* for in its mysterious lumination nothing cast a shadow. A shallow pool in the guttered depression of an old wheel rut, as from a recent rain, met his eye with a crimson gleam. He *stooped* and *plunged* his hand into it. It stained his fingers; it was blood! Blood, he then observed, was about him everywhere. The weeds growing rankly by the roadside showed it in blots and

---

Fatigue - *Tiredness*
Upright - *Erect*
Perfunctory - *Superficial*
Whence - *From what place, where*
Conspiracy - *Plotting*
Diffusion - *Verbosity*
Plunged - *To thrust forcible or suddenly*

splashes on their big, broad leaves. Patches of dry dust between the wheel-ways were pitted and spattered as with a red rain. ***Defiling*** the trunks of the trees were broad maculations of crimson, and blood dripped like dew from their foliage.

All this he observed with a terror which seemed not incompatible with the fulfilment of a natural expectation. It seemed to him that it was all in ***expiation*** of some crime which, though conscious of his guilt, he could not rightly remember. To the menaces and mysteries of his surroundings the consciousness was an added horror. Vainly he sought, by tracing life backward in memory, to reproduce the moment of his sin; scenes and incidents came crowding ***tumultuously*** into his mind, one picture effacing another, or ***commingling*** with it in confusion and obscurity, but nowhere could he catch a glimpse of what he sought. The failure ***augmented*** his terror; he felt as one who has murdered in the dark, not knowing whom nor why. So frightful was the situation -- the mysterious light burned with so silent and awful a ***menace***; the noxious plants, the trees that by common consent are invested with a melancholy or baleful character, so openly in his sight conspired against his peace; from overhead and all about came so audible and startling whispers and the sighs of creatures so obviously not of earth -- that he could endure it no longer, and with a great effort to break some ***malign*** spell that bound his faculties to silence and inaction, he shouted with the full strength of his lungs! His voice, broken, it seemed, into an infinite multitude of unfamiliar sounds, went babbling and stammering away into the distant reaches of the forest, died into silence, and all was as before. But he had made a beginning at resistance and was encouraged. He said:

'I will not submit unheard. There may be powers that are not malignant travelling this accursed road. I shall leave them a record and an appeal. I shall relate my wrongs, the persecutions that I endure -- I, a helpless mortal, a penitent, an ***unoffending*** poet!' Halpin Frayser was a poet only as he was a penitent: in his dream.

Taking from his clothing a small red-leather pocket-book one half of which was leaved for ***memoranda***, he discovered that he was without a pencil. He broke a twig from a bush, dipped it into a pool of blood and wrote rapidly. He had hardly touched the paper with the point of his twig when a low, wild peal of

Defiling - *Making a narrow passage*
Expiation - *Atonement*
Tumultuously - *Highly agitated*
Commingling - *Combining, blending*
Augmented - *To make larger*
Memoranda - *A record, a written statement*

laughter broke out at a measureless distance away, and growing ever louder, seemed approaching ever nearer; a soulless, heartless, and unjoyous laugh, like that of the loon, solitary by the lakeside at midnight; a laugh which culminated in an unearthly shout close at hand, then died away by slow *gradations*, as if the *accursed* being that uttered it had withdrawn over the verge of the world whence it had come. But the man felt that this was not so -- that it was near by and had not moved.

A strange sensation began slowly to take possession of his body and his mind. He could not have said which, if any, of his senses was affected; he felt it rather as a consciousness -- a mysterious mental assurance of some overpowering presence -- some supernatural *malevolence* different in kind from the invisible existences that swarmed about him, and superior to them in power. He knew that it had uttered that hideous laugh. And now it seemed to be approaching him; from what direction he did not know -- dared not *conjecture*. All his former fears were forgotten or merged in the gigantic terror that now held him in thrall. Apart from that, he had but one thought: to complete his written appeal to the benign powers who, traversing the haunted wood, might sometime rescue him if he should be denied the blessing of *annihilation*. He wrote with terrible rapidity, the twig in his fingers *rilling* blood without renewal; but in the middle of a sentence his hands denied their service to his will, his arms fell to his sides, the book to the earth; and powerless to move or cry out, he found himself staring into the sharply drawn face and blank, dead eyes of his own mother, standing white and silent in the garments of the grave!

II

In his youth Halpin Frayser had lived with his parents in Nashville, Tennessee. The Fraysers were well-to-do, having a good position in such society as had survived the wreck wrought by civil war. Their children had the social and educational opportunities of their time and place, and had responded to good associations and instruction with agreeable manners and cultivated minds. Halpin being the youngest and not over robust was perhaps a trifle 'spoiled.' He had the double disadvantage of a mother's *assiduity* and a father's neglect. Frayser pere was what no Southern man of means is not -- a politician. His coun-

Gradations - *Stages or degrees*
Accursed - *Ill-fated*
Annihilation - *Extinction, destruction*
Assiduity - *Devoted attention*

try, or rather his section and State, made demands upon his time and attention so *exacting* that to those of his family he was *compelled* to turn an ear partly *deafened* by the thunder of the political captains and the shouting, his own included.

Young Halpin was of a dreamy, indolent and rather romantic turn, somewhat more addicted to literature than law, the profession to which he was bred. Among those of his relations who professed the modern faith of heredity it was well understood that in him the character of the late Myron Bayne, a maternal great-grandfather, had revisited the glimpses of the moon -- by which orb Bayne had in his lifetime been sufficiently affected to be a poet of no small Colonial distinction. If not specially observed, it was observable that while a Frayser who was not the proud possessor of a *sumptuous* copy of the ancestral 'poetical works' (printed at the family expense, and long ago withdrawn from an inhospitable market) was a rare Frayser indeed, there was an illogical indisposition to honour the great deceased in the person of his spiritual successor. Halpin was pretty generally *deprecated* as an intellectual black sheep who was likely at any moment to disgrace the flock by bleating in metre. The Tennessee Fraysers were a practical folk -- not practical in the popular sense of devotion to *sordid pursuits*, but having a robust contempt for any qualities *unfitting* a man for the wholesome vocation of politics.

In justice to young Halpin it should be said that while in him were pretty faithfully reproduced most of the mental and moral characteristics ascribed by history and family tradition to the famous Colonial bard, his succession to the gift and faculty divine was purely *inferential*. Not only had he never been known to court the Muse, but in truth he could not have written correctly a line of verse to save himself from the Killer of the Wise. Still, there was no knowing when the dormant faculty might wake and *smite* the *lyre*.

In the meantime the young man was rather a loose fish, anyhow. Between him and his mother was the most perfect sympathy, for secretly the lady was herself a *devout* disciple of the late and great Myron Bayne, though with the tact so generally and justly admired in her sex (despite the hardy *calumniators* who insist that it is essentially the same thing as cunning) she had always taken care to conceal her weakness from all eyes but those of him who shared it. Their

Sumptuous - *Luxurious*
Deprecated - *To express earnest disapproval*
Sordid - *Selfish*
Inferential - *Pertaining to*
Smite - *To hit hard*
Lyre - *A musical instrument*
Calumniators - *People making false statements*

common guilt in respect of that was an added tie between them. If in Halpin's youth his mother had 'spoiled' him he had assuredly done his part toward being spoiled. As he grew to such manhood as is *attainable* by a Southerner who does not care which way elections go, the attachment between him and his beautiful mother -- whom from early childhood he had called Katy -- became yearly stronger and more tender. In these two romantic natures was manifest in a signal way that neglected phenomenon, the dominance of the sexual element in all the relations of life, strengthening, softening, and beautifying even those of consanguinity. The two were nearly inseparable, and by strangers observing their manners were not infrequently mistaken for lovers.

Entering his mother's boudoir one day Halpin Frayser kissed her upon the forehead, toyed for a moment with a lock of her dark hair which had escaped from its confining pins, and said, with an obvious effort at calmness:

'Would you greatly mind, Katy, if I were called away to California for a few weeks?'

It was hardly needful for Katy to answer with her lips a question to which her tell-tale cheeks had made instant reply. Evidently she would greatly mind; and the tears, too, sprang into her large brown eyes as *corroborative testimony.*

'Ah, my son,' she said, looking up into his face with infinite tenderness,' I should have known that this was coming. Did I not lie awake a half of the night weeping because, during the other half, Grandfather Bayne had come to me in a dream, and standing by his portrait -- young, too, and handsome as that -- pointed to yours on the same wall? And when I looked it seemed that I could not see the features; you had been painted with a face cloth, such as we put upon the dead. Your father has laughed at me, but you and I, dear, know that such things are not for nothing. And I saw below the edge of the cloth the marks of hands on your throat -- forgive me, but we have not been used to keep such things from each other. Perhaps you have another *interpretation*. Perhaps it does not mean that you will go to California. Or maybe you will take me with you?'

It must be confessed that this *ingenious* interpretation of the dream in the light of newly discovered evidence did not wholly *commend* itself to the son's more logical mind; he had, for the moment at least, a *conviction* that it foreshadowed a

---

Attainable - *Achievable*
Corroborative - *Confirmative*
Testimony - *A statement of declartion*
Interpretation - *Explanation*
Ingenious - *Bright, gifted*
Cmmend - *Praisen*

more simple and immediate, if less tragic, disaster than a visit to the Pacific Coast. It was Halpin Frayser's impression that he was to be *garroted* on his native heath.

'Are there not medicinal springs in California?' Mrs. Frayser resumed before he had time to give her the true reading of the dream -- 'places where one recovers from rheumatism and *neuralgia*? Look -- my fingers feel so stiff; and I am almost sure they have been giving me great pain while I slept.' She held out her hands for his inspection. What *diagnosis* of her case the young man may have thought it best to conceal with a smile the historian is unable to state, but for himself he feels bound to say that fingers looking less stiff, and showing fewer evidences of even insensible pain, have seldom been submitted for medical inspection by even the fairest patient desiring a prescription of unfamiliar scenes. The outcome of it was that of these two odd persons having equally odd notions of duty, the one went to California, as the interest of his client required, and the other remained at home in compliance with a wish that her husband was scarcely conscious of entertaining.

While in San Francisco Halpin Frayser was walking one dark night along the water-front of the city, when, with a suddenness that surprised and disconcerted him, he became a sailor. He was in fact '*shanghaied*' aboard a gallant, gallant ship, and sailed for a far countree. Nor did his misfortunes end with the voyage; for the ship was cast ashore on an island of the South Pacific, and it was six years afterward when the survivors were taken off by a venturesome trading schooner and brought back to San Francisco.

Though poor in purse, Frayser was no less proud in spirit than he had been in the years that seemed ages and ages ago. He would accept no assistance from strangers, and it was while living with a fellow survivor near the town of St. Helena, awaiting news and *remittances* from home, that he had gone gunning and dreaming.

III

The apparition *confronting* the dreamer in the haunted wood -- the thing so like, yet so unlike, his mother -- was horrible! It stirred no love nor *longings* insis heart; it came unattended with pleasant memories of a golden past --

Garroted - *To execute by the garrote, throttle*
Neuralgia - *Sever pain due to nerve damage*
Diagnosis - *Determining*
Shanghaied - *To kidnap*
Remittances - *Sending of money*
Confronting - *Opposing*

inspired no sentiment of any kind; all the finer emotions were swallowed up in fear. He tried to turn and run from before it, but his legs were as lead; he was unable to lift his feet from the ground. His arms hung helpless at his sides; of his eyes only he retained control, and these he dared not remove from the *lustreless* orbs of the apparition, which he knew was not a soul without a body, but that most dreadful of all existences *infesting* that haunted wood -- a body without a soul! In its blank stare was neither love, nor pity, nor intelligence -- nothing to which to address an appeal for mercy. 'An appeal will not lie,' he thought, with an absurd reversion to professional slang, making the situation more horrible, as the fire of a cigar might light up a tomb.

For a time, which seemed so long that the world grew grey with age and sin, and the haunted forest, having fulfilled its purpose in this monstrous *culmination* of its terrors, vanished out of his consciousness with all its sights and sounds, the apparition stood within a pace, regarding him with the mindless *malevolence* of a wild brute; then thrust its hands forward and sprang upon him with *appalling ferocity*! The act released his physical energies without unfettering his will; his mind was still spellbound, but his powerful body and agile limbs, *endowed* with a blind, insensate life of their own, resisted *stoutly* and well. For an instant he seemed to see this unnatural contest between a dead intelligence and a breathing mechanism only as a spectator -- such fancies are in dreams; then he regained his identity almost as if by a leap forward into his body, and the straining automaton had a directing will as alert and fierce as that of its hideous antagonist.

But what mortal can cope with a creature of his dream? The imagination creating the enemy is already vanquished; the combat's result is the combat's cause. Despite his struggles -- despite his strength and activity, which seemed wasted in a void, he felt the cold fingers close upon his throat. Borne backward to the earth, he saw above him the dead and drawn face within a hand's-breadth of his own, and then all was black. A sound as of the beating of distant drums -- a murmur of *swarming* voices, a sharp, far cry signing all to silence, and Halpin Frayser dreamed that he was dead.

Lustreless - *Without sheen, dull*
Infesting - *Inhabit, overrun*
Culmination - *Result, ending*
Appalling - *Causing dismay or horror*
Stoutly - *Bravely*
Swarming - *To hover, congregate*

IV

A warm, clear night had been followed by a morning of *drenching* fog. At about the middle of the afternoon of the preceding day a little whiff of light vapour -- a mere thickening of the atmosphere, the ghost of a cloud -- had been observed *clinging* to the western side of Mount St. Helena, away up along the barren altitudes near the summit. It was so thin, so *diaphanous*, so like a fancy made visible, that one would have said: 'Look quickly! in a moment it will be gone.' In a moment it was visibly larger and denser. While with one edge it clung to the mountain, with the other it reached farther and farther out into the air above the lower slopes. At the same time it extended itself to north and south, joining small patches of mist that appeared to come out of the mountain-side on exactly the same level, with an intelligent design to be absorbed. And so it grew and grew until the summit was shut out of view from the valley, and over the valley itself was an ever-extending *canopy, opaque* and grey. At Calistoga, which lies near the head of the valley and the foot of the mountain, there were a starless night and a sunless morning. The fog, sinking into the valley, had reached southward, swallowing up ranch after ranch, until it had blotted out the town of St. Helena, nine miles away. The dust in the road was laid; trees were adrip with moisture; birds sat silent in their *coverts*; the morning light was wan and *ghastly*, with neither colour nor fire.

Two men left the town of St. Helena at the first glimmer of dawn, and walked along the road north-ward up the valley toward Calistoga. They carried guns on their shoulders, yet no one having knowledge of such matters could have mistaken them for hunters of bird or beast. They were a deputy sheriff from Napa and a detective from San Francisco -- Holker and Jaralson, respectively. Their business was man-hunting.

'How far is it?' inquired Holker, as they strode along, their feet stirring white the dust beneath the damp surface of the road.

'The White Church? Only a half mile farther,' the other answered. 'By the way,' he added, 'it is neither white nor a church; it is an abandoned schoolhouse, grey with age and neglect. Religious services were once held in it -- when it was

Drenching - *To get wet thoroughly*
Diaphanous - *Completely transparently*
Canopy - *a covering*
Coverts - *Disguised*
Ghastly - *Terrible*

white, and there is a graveyard that would delight a poet. Can you guess why I sent for you, and told you to come armed?'

'Oh, I never have bothered you about things of that kind. I've always found you communicative when the time came. But if I may hazard a guess, you want me to help you arrest one of the corpses in the graveyard.'

'You remember Branscom?' said Jaralson, treating his companion's wit with the *inattention* that it deserved.

'The chap who cut his wife's throat? I ought; I wasted a week's work on him and had my expenses for my trouble. There is a reward of five hundred dollars, but none of us ever got a sight of him. You don't mean to say -- '

'Yes, I do. He has been under the noses of you fellows all the time. He comes by night to the old graveyard at the White Church.'

'The devil! That's where they buried his wife.'

'Well, you fellows might have had sense enough to suspect that he would return to her grave some time!'

'The very last place that anyone would have expected him to return to.'

'But you had exhausted all the other places. Learning your failure at them, I "laid for him" there.'

'And you found him?'

'Damn it! he found me. The rascal got the drop on me -- regularly held me up and made me travel. It's God's mercy that he didn't go through me. Oh, he's a good one, and I fancy the half of that reward is enough for me if you're needy.'

Holker laughed good-humouredly, and explained that his *creditors* were never more *importunate*.

'I wanted merely to show you the ground, and arrange a plan with you,' the detective explained. 'I thought it as well for us to be armed, even in daylight.'

'The man must be *insane*,' said the deputy sheriff. 'The reward is for his capture and *conviction*. If he's mad he won't be convicted.'

Mr. Holker was so profoundly affected by that possible failure of justice that he involuntarily stopped in the middle of the road, then resumed his walk with *abated zeal*.

'Well, he looks it,' *assented* Jaralson. 'I'm bound to admit that a more *unshaven, unshorn, unkempt*, and uneverything

Creditors - *Persons or firms to whom money is due*
Importunate - *Urgent*
Insane - *Mad*
Abated -*To lessen*
Unshorn - *Unshaven*
Unkempt - *Uncared, neglected*

wretch I never saw outside the ancient and honourable order of tramps. But I've gone in for him, and can't make up my mind to let go. There's glory in it for us, anyhow. Not another soul knows that he is this side of the Mountains of the Moon.'

'All right,' Holker said; 'we will go and view the ground,' and he added, in the words of a once favourite inscription for tombstones: '"where you must shortly lie" -- I mean if old Branscom ever gets tired of you and your *impertinent intrusion*. By the way, I heard the other day that "Branscom" was not his real name.'

'What is?'

'I can't recall it. I had lost all interest in the wretch and it did not fix itself in my memory -- something like Pardee. The woman whose throat he had the bad taste to cut was a widow when he met her. She had come to California to look up some relatives -- there are persons who will do that sometimes. But you know all that.'

'Naturally.' 'But not knowing the right name, by what happy inspiration did you find the right grave? The man who told me what the name was said it had been cut on the headboard.'

'I don't know the right grave.' Jaralson was apparently a *trifle reluctant* to admit his ignorance of so important a point of his plan. 'I have been watching about the place generally. A part of our work this morning will be to identify that grave. Here is the White Church.'

For a long distance the road had been bordered by fields on both sides, but now on the left there was a forest of oaks, madronos, and gigantic **spruces** whose lower parts only could be seen, dim and ghostly in the fog. The undergrowth was, in places, thick, but nowhere impenetrable. For some moments Holker saw nothing of the building, but as they turned into the woods it revealed itself in faint grey outline through the fog, looking huge and far away. A few steps more, and it was within an arm's length, distinct, dark with moisture, and insignificant in size. It had the usual country-schoolhouse form -- belonged to the packing-box order of architecture; had an **underpinning** of stones, a moss-grown roof, and blank window spaces, whence both glass and sash had long departed. It was ruined, but not a ruin -- a typical Californian substitute for what are known to guide-bookers

Impertinent - *Irrelevant entry*
Intrusion - *A forceful*
Trifle - *A thing*
Reluctant - *Unwilling*
Spruces - *Evergreen coniferous trees*
Underpinning - *Of little value*

abroad as 'monuments of the past.' With scarcely a glance at this uninteresting structure Jaralson moved on into the dripping undergrowth beyond.

'I will show you where he held me up,' he said. 'This is the graveyard.'

Here and there among the bushes were small ***enclosures*** containing graves, sometimes no more than one. They were recognised as graves by the discoloured stones or rotting boards at head and foot, ***leaning*** at all angles, some prostrate; by the ruined picket fences surrounding them; or, infrequently, by the mound itself showing its gravel through the fallen leaves. In many instances nothing marked the spot where lay the vestiges of some poor ***mortal*** -- who, leaving 'a large circle of sorrowing friends,' had been left by them in turn -- except a depression in the earth, more lasting than that in the spirits of the mourners. The paths, if any paths had been, were long obliterated; trees of a considerable size had been permitted to grow up from the graves and thrust aside with root or branch the ***enclosing*** fences. Over all was that air of abandonment and decay which seems nowhere so fit and significant as in a village of the forgotten dead.

As the two men, Jaralson leading, pushed their way through the growth of young trees, that ***enterprising*** man suddenly stopped and brought up his shotgun to the height of his breast, uttered a low note of warning, and stood motionless, his eyes fixed upon something ahead. As well as he could, ***obstructed*** by brush, his companion, though seeing nothing, imitated the posture and so stood, prepared for what might ensue. A moment later Jaralson moved ***cautiously*** forward, the other following.

Under the branches of an enormous spruce lay the dead body of a man. Standing silent above it they noted such particulars as first strike the attention -- the face, the attitude, the clothing; whatever most promptly and plainly answers the unspoken question of a sympathetic curiosity. The body lay upon its back, the legs wide apart. One arm was thrust upward, the other outward; but the latter was bent acutely, and the hand was near the throat. Both hands were tightly ***clenched***. The whole attitude was that of desperate but ***ineffectual resistance*** to -- what?

Near by lay a shotgun and a game bag through the meshes of which was seen the ***plumage*** of shot birds. All about were

Enclosures - *Fencing*
Mortal - *Subject death*
Enterprising - *Resourceful, adventurous*
Clenched - *Grasped firmly*
Plumage - *Feathers collectively*

evidences of a furious struggle; small sprouts of poison-oak were bent and *denuded* of leaf and bark; dead and rotting leaves had been pushed into heaps and ridges on both sides of the legs by the action of other feet than theirs; alongside the hips were unmistakable impressions of human knees.

The nature of the struggle was made clear by a glance at the dead man's throat and face. While breast and hands were white, those were purple -- almost black. The shoulders lay upon a low mound, and the head was turned back at an angle otherwise impossible, the expanded eyes staring blankly backward in a direction opposite to that of the feet. From the froth filling the open mouth the tongue *protruded*, black and swollen. The throat showed horrible *contusions*; not mere finger-marks, but *bruises* and *lacerations* wrought by two strong hands that must have buried themselves in the yielding flesh, maintaining their terrible grasp until long after death. Breast, throat, face, were wet; the clothing was saturated; drops of water, *condensed* from the fog, studded the hair and moustache.

All this the two men observed without speaking -- almost at a glance. Then Holker said:

'Poor devil! he had a rough deal.'

Jaralson was making a *vigilant circumspection* of the forest, his shotgun held in both hands and at full cock, his finger upon the trigger.

'The work of a *maniac*,' he said, without withdrawing his eyes from the enclosing wood. 'It was done by Branscom -- Pardee.'

Something half hidden by the disturbed leaves on the earth caught Holker's attention. It was a redleather pocketbook. He picked it up and opened it. It contained leaves of white paper for *memoranda*, and upon the first leaf was the name 'Halpin Frayser.' Written in red on several succeeding leaves -- scrawled as if in haste and barely *legible* -- were the following lines, which Holker read aloud, while his companion continued *scanning* the dim grey confines of their narrow world and hearing matter of apprehension in the drip of water from every burdened branch:

> '*Enthralled* by some mysterious spell, I stood
> In the lit gloom of an enchanted wood.

Protruded - *Bulged, thrust forwards*
Bruises - *Slight injuries*
Lacerations - *Jagged wounds or outs*
Circumspection - *Cautious careful*
Maniac - *Crazy*
Scanning - *Examining*
Enthralled - *Captivated charmed*

The cypress there and myrtle twined their ***boughs***,
Significant, in ***baleful*** brotherhood.
'The brooding willow whispered to the yew;
Beneath, the deadly nightshade and the rue,
With ***immortelles*** self-woven into strange
Funereal shapes, and horrid nettles grew.
'No song of bird nor any drone of bees,
Nor light leaf lifted by the wholesome breeze:
The air was stagnant all, and Silence was
A living thing that breathed among the trees.
'***Conspiring*** spirits whispered in the gloom,
Half-heard, the stilly secrets of the tomb.
With blood the trees were all adrip; the leaves
Shone in the witch-light with a ***ruddy*** bloom.
'I cried aloud! -- the spell, unbroken still,
Rested upon my spirit and my will.
Unsouled, unhearted, hopeless and forlorn,
I strove with monstrous ***presages*** of ill!
'At last the viewless -- '

Holker ceased reading; there was no more to read. The manuscript broke off in the middle of a line.

'That sounds like Bayne,' said Jaralson, who was something of a scholar in his way. He had ***abated*** his vigilance and stood looking down at the body.

'Who's Bayne?' Holker asked rather incuriously.

'Myron Bayne, a chap who flourished in the early years of the nation -- more than a century ago. Wrote mighty dismal stuff; I have his collected works. That poem is not among them, but it must have been omitted by mistake.'

'It is cold,' said Holker; 'let us leave here; we must have up the coroner from Napa.'

Jaralson said nothing, but made a movement in compliance. Passing the end of the slight elevation of earth upon which the dead man's head and shoulders lay, his foot struck some hard substance under the rotting forest leaves, and he took the trouble to kick it into view. It was a fallen headboard, and painted on it were the hardly ***decipherable*** words, 'Catharine Larue.'

Funereal - *Mournful, gloomy*
Conspiring - *Plotting against*
Presages - *Prophetic*
Ruddy - *Damned*
Decipherable - *To interpret, depictable, portrayable*

'Larue, Larue!' exclaimed Holker, with sudden animation. 'Why, that is the real name of Branscom -- not Pardee. And -- bless my soul! how it all comes to me -- the murdered woman's name had been Frayser!'

'There is some rascally mystery here,' said Detective Jaralson. 'I hate anything of that kind.' There came to them out of the fog -- seemingly from a great distance -- the sound of a laugh, a low, *deliberate*, soulless laugh which had no more of joy than that of a hyena *night-prowling* in the desert; a laugh that rose by slow gradation, louder and louder, clearer, more distinct and terrible, until it seemed barely outside the narrow circle of their vision; a laugh so unnatural, so unhuman, so *devilish*, that it filled those hardy man-hunters with a sense of dread *unspeakable*! They did not move their weapons nor think of them; the menace of that horrible sound was not of the kind to be met with arms. As it had grown out of silence, so now it died away; from a *culminating* shout which had seemed almost in their ears, it drew itself away into the distance until its failing notes, joyous and *mechanical* to the last, sank to silence at a measureless remove.

Food For Thought

Some literary critics feel that the ending of this story is very sporadic and confusing. How do you feel about it? Do you think that the story could have a better ending? Suggest one suitable ending of this story, using your own imaginative skills.

Deliberate -
Night - Prowling -
Devilish -
Unspeakable -
Mechanical -

An Understanding

Q. 1. Who was Halpin Frayser and where did he live? How and why was he forced to work as a sailor during his trip to California?
Ans. _____
_____
_____
_____
_____

Q. 2. Whom did Halpin Frayser loved the most? How was his life after being marooned on an island far away from his home? Describe the mental state of Frayser briefly in your own words.
Ans. _____
_____
_____
_____
_____

Q. 3. Why does the author feel that there are glaring differences between joining as a sailor or a soldier on one's own will and wish and being forced to join as a sailor or a soldier? Do you think that Frayser missed his mother and his loved ones and this was one of the many reasons that culminated into his death?
Ans. _____
_____
_____
_____
_____

Q. 4. What did Halpin Frayser do and how was his life when he lived with his parents in Nashville, Tennessee? What was his family background and lifestyle before becoming a sailor?
Ans. _____
_____
_____
_____
_____

The Striding Place
—Gertrude Atherton

WEigall, continental and detached, tired early of grouse shooting. To stand propped against a sod fence while his host's workmen *routed* up the birds with long poles and drove them towards the waiting guns, made him feel himself a parody on the ancestors who had roamed the moors and forests of this West Riding of Yorkshire in hot *pursuit* of game worth the killing. But when in England in August he always accepted whatever *proffered* for the season, and invited his host to shoot *pheasants* on his estates in the South. The amusements of life, he argued, should be accepted with the same philosophy as its ills.

It had been a bad day. A heavy rain had made the *moor* so spongy that it fairly sprang beneath the feet. Whether or not the grouse had haunts of their own, wherein they were immune from *rheumatism*, the bag had been small. The women, too, were an unusually dull lot, with the exception of a new-minded *debutante* who bothered Weigall at dinner by demanding the verbal restoration of the vague paintings on the vaulted roof above them.

But it was no one of these things that sat on Weigall's mind as, when the other men went up to bed, he let himself out of the castle and *sauntered* down to the river. His intimate friend, the companion of his boyhood, the *chum* of his college days, his fellow-traveller in many lands, the man for whom he possessed stronger affection than for all men, had mysteriously disappeared two days ago, and his track might have sprung to the upper air for all trace he had left behind him. He had been a guest on the adjoining estate during the past week, shooting with the fervor of the true sportsman, making love in the intervals to Adeline Cavan, and apparently in the best of spirits. As far as was known there was nothing to lower his mental mercury, for his rent-roll was a large one, Miss Cavan blushed whenever he looked at her, and, being one of the best shots in England, he was never happier than in August. The suicide theory was *preposterous*, all agreed, and there was as little reason to believe him murdered. Nevertheless, he had walked out of March Abbey two nights ago without hat or overcoat, and had not been seen since.

The country was being *patrolled* night and day. A hundred keepers and workmen were beating the woods and *poking* the

Routed - *Overwhelming defeat*
Proffered - *Proposed, suggested*
Pheasants - *A type of long-tailed birds*
Moor - *A tract or open land*
Rheumatism - *A type of bone problem*
Debutante - *A young woman making debut into the society*
Sauntered - *A leisure walk*

bogs on the moors, but as yet not so much as a handkerchief had been found.

Weigall did not believe for a moment that Wyatt Gifford was dead, and although it was impossible not to be affected by the general uneasiness, he was disposed to be more angry than frightened. At Cambridge Gifford had been an incorrigible practical joker, and by no means had outgrown the habit; it would be like him to cut across the country in his evening clothes, board a cattle-train, and *amuse* himself touching up the picture of the sensation in West Riding.

However, Weigall's affection for his friend was too deep to companion with tranquillity in the present state of doubt, and, instead of going to bed early with the other men, he determined to walk until ready for sleep. He went down to the river and followed the path through the woods. There was no moon, but the stars *sprinkled* their cold light upon the pretty belt of water flowing *placidly* past wood and ruin, between green masses of overhanging rocks or sloping banks tangled with tree and shrub, leaping occasionally over stones with the harsh notes of an angry scold, to recover its *equanimity* the moment the way was clear again.

It was very dark in the depths where Weigall trod. He smiled as he recalled a remark of Gifford's: "An English wood is like a good many other things in life -- very promising at a distance, but a hollow mockery when you get within. You see daylight on both sides, and the sun freckles the very *bracken*. Our woods need the night to make them seem what they ought to be -- what they once were, before our ancestors' *descendants* demanded so much more money, in these so much more various days."

Weigall *strolled* along, smoking, and thinking of his friend, his pranks -- many of which had done more credit to his imagination than this -- and recalling conversations that had lasted the night through. Just before the end of the London season they had walked the streets one hot night after a party, discussing the various theories of the soul's destiny. That afternoon they had met at the coffin of a college friend whose mind had been a blank for the past three years. Some months previously they had called at the asylum to see him. His expression had been senile, his face *imprinted* with the record of *debauchery*. In death the face was placid, intelligent, without *ignoble lineation* -- the face of the man they had known at college. Weigall and Gifford had had no time to comment there, and the afternoon and

Sprinkled - *Scattered*
Placidly - *Peaceful*
Equanimity - *Mental stability*
Bracken - *A cluster of ferns*
Ignoble - *Of low character*

evening were full; but, coming forth from the house of festivity together, they had reverted almost at once to the topic.

"I cherish the theory," Gifford had said, "that the soul sometimes *lingers* in the body after death. During madness, of course, it is an *impotent* prisoner, albeit a conscious one. Fancy its agony, and its horror! What more natural than that, when the life-spark goes out, the tortured soul should take possession of the vacant skull and triumph once more for a few hours while old friends look their last? It has had time to repent while *compelled* to crouch and behold the result of its work, and it has shrived itself into a state of comparative purity. If I had my way, I should stay inside my bones until the coffin had gone into its *niche*, that I might obviate for my poor old comrade the tragic impersonality of death. And I should like to see justice done to it, as it were -- to see it lowered among its ancestors with the ceremony and *solemnity* that are its due. I am afraid that if I dissevered myself too quickly, I should yield to curiosity and hasten to investigate the mysteries of space."

"You believe in the soul as an independent *entity*, then -- that it and the vital principle are not one and the same?"

"Absolutely. The body and soul are twins, life *comrades* -- sometimes friends, sometimes enemies, but always loyal in the last instance. Some day, when I am tired of the world, I shall go to India and become a mahatma, solely for the pleasure of receiving proof during life of this independent relationship."

"Suppose you were not sealed up properly, and returned after one of your astral flights to find your earthly part unfit for habitation? It is an experiment I don't think I should care to try, unless even *juggling* with soul and flesh had palled."

"That would not be an uninteresting *predicament*. I should rather enjoy experimenting with broken machinery."

The high wild roar of water smote suddenly upon Weigall's ear and checked his memories. He left the wood and walked out on the huge slippery stones which nearly close the River Wharfe at this point, and watched the waters boil down into the narrow pass with their furious untiring energy. The black quiet of the woods rose high on either side. The stars seemed colder and whiter just above. On either hand the perspective of the river might have run into a *rayless cavern*. There was no lonelier spot in England, nor one which had the right to claim so many ghosts, if ghosts there were.

Lingers - *To remain alive, persist*
Impotent - *Lacking power or ability*
Niche - *A recess in a wall*
Solemnity - *Earnestness*
Entity - *Existence*
Comrades - *Companion*
Juggling - *To perform magical tricks*
Predicament - *A difficult situation*

Weigall was not a coward, but he recalled uncomfortably the tales of those that had been done to death in the Strid: Wordsworth's Boy of Egremond had been disposed of by the practical Whitaker; but countless others, more **venturesome** than wise, had gone down into that narrow boiling course, never to appear in the still pool a few yards beyond. Below the great rocks which form the walls of the Strid was believed to be a natural **vault**, on to whose shelves the dead were drawn. The spot had an ugly fascination. Weigall stood, visioning skeletons, uncoffined and green, the home of the eyeless things which had devoured all that had covered and filled that **rattling** symbol of man's mortality; then fell to wondering if any one had attempted to leap the Strid of late. It was covered with slime; he had never seen it look so **treacherous**.

He shuddered and turned away, impelled, despite his manhood, to flee the spot. As he did so, something tossing in the foam below the fall -- something as white, yet independent of it -- caught his eye and arrested his step. Then he saw that it was describing a contrary motion to the rushing water -- an upward backward motion. Weigall stood rigid, breathless; he fancied he heard the crackling of his hair. Was that a hand? It thrust itself still higher above the boiling **foam**, turned sidewise, and four frantic fingers were distinctly visible against the black rock beyond.

Weigall's superstitious terror left him. A man was there, struggling to free himself from the **suction** beneath the Strid, swept down, doubtless, but a moment before his arrival, perhaps as he stood with his back to the current.

He stepped as close to the edge as he dared. The hand doubled as if in **imprecation**, shaking savagely in the face of that force which leaves its creatures to **immutable** law; then spread wide again, **clutching**, expanding, crying for help as audibly as the human voice.

Weigall dashed to the nearest tree, dragged and twisted off a branch with his strong arms, and returned as swiftly to the Strid. The hand was in the same place, still **gesticulating** as wildly; the body was undoubtedly caught in the rocks below, perhaps already half-way along one of those hideous shelves. Weigall let himself down upon a lower rock, braced his shoulder against the mass beside him, then, **leaning** out over the water, thrust the branch into the hand. The fingers clutched it **convulsively**. Weigall tugged powerfully, his own feet dragged **perilously** near the edge. For a moment he produced no impression, then an arm shot above the waters.

Vault - *An arched structure*
Treacherous - *Deceptive*
Suction - *The process of sucking*
Imprecation - *A curse*
Immutable - *Unchangeable*

The blood sprang to Weigall's head; he was **choked** with the impression that the Strid had him in her roaring hold, and he saw nothing. Then the mist cleared. The hand and arm were nearer, although the rest of the body was still **concealed** by the foam. Weigall peered out with distended eyes. The meagre light *revealed* in the cuffs links of a peculiar device. The fingers clutching the branch were as familiar.

Weigall forgot the slippery stones, the terrible death if he stepped too far. He pulled with passionate will and muscle. Memories flung themselves into the hot light of his brain, ***trooping*** rapidly upon each other's heels, as in the thought of the drowning. Most of the pleasures of his life, good and bad, were identified in some way with this friend. Scenes of college days, of travel, where they had deliberately sought adventure and stood between one another and death upon more occasions than one, of hours of delightful companionship among the treasures of art, and others in the pursuit of pleasure, flashed like the changing particles of a kaleidoscope. Weigall had loved several women; but he would have flouted in these moments the thought that he had ever loved any woman as he loved Wyatt Gifford. There were so many charming women in the world, and in the thirty-two years of his life he had never known another man to whom he had cared to give his intimate friendship.

He threw himself on his face. His wrists were cracking, the skin was torn from his hands. The fingers still ***gripped*** the stick. There was life in them yet.

Suddenly something gave way. The hand swung about, tearing the branch from Weigall's grasp. The body had been liberated and flung outward, though still submerged by the foam and spray.

Weigall ***scrambled*** to his feet and sprang along the rocks, knowing that the danger from suction was over and that Gifford must be carried straight to the quiet pool. Gifford was a fish in the water and could live under it longer than most men. If he survived this, it would not be the first time that his pluck and science had saved him from drowning.

Weigall reached the pool. A man in his evening clothes floated on it, his face turned towards a projecting rock over which his arm had fallen, ***upholding*** the body. The hand that had held the branch hung limply over the rock, its white reflection visible in the black water. Weigall plunged into the shallow pool, lifted Gifford in his arms and returned to the bank. He laid the body down and threw

Choked - *Strangle*
Concealed - *Tide*
Revealed - *Exposed*
Trooping - *Gathering persons/things*
Gripped - *Grasped, seized*

off his coat that he might be the freer to practise the methods of *resuscitation*. He was glad of the moment's *respite*. The valiant life in the man might have been exhausted in that last struggle. He had not dared to look at his face, to put his ear to the heart. The hesitation lasted but a moment. There was no time to lose.

He turned to his prostrate friend. As he did so, something strange and disagreeable smote his senses. For a half-moment he did not *appreciate* its nature. Then his teeth cracked together, his feet, his outstretched arms pointed towards the woods. But he sprang to the side of the man and bent down and peered into his face. There was no face.

> "This striding place is called the 'Strid,'
>
> A name which it took of yore;
>
> A thousand years hath it borne the name,
>
> And it shall a thousand more."

Food For Thought

Weigall recognised his friend, Gifford's hand waving in the water, who had disappeared two days back. When he jumped into the water and lifted the body - the body began to gain consciousness, but had no face. What do you think was it? Give reasons for your answer.

Resuscitation - *To revive, restore consciousness*
Respite - *Relieve temporarily*
Appreciate - *Applaud*

An Understanding

Q. 1. Where do Weigall and his friends go for grouse hunting every year? What happened to one of his friends, who mysteriously disappeared this time?

Ans. _____
_____
_____
_____
_____

Q. 2. What did Weigall hear and see as he walked around the peaceful woods in the star-studded night?

Ans. _____
_____
_____
_____
_____

Q. 3. After hearing the roar of the river, what did Weigall suddenly remember? Which place was considered to be the loneliest place in England and what did Weigall see there?

Ans. _____
_____
_____
_____
_____

Q. 4. Weigall recognised the hand waving in the river water. Whose hand was it and what happened next? Narrate the incident that followed briefly in your own words.

Ans. _____
_____
_____
_____
_____

SELF-IMPROVEMENT/PERSONALITY DEVELOPMENT

      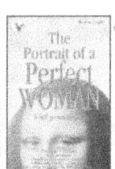 

All books available at **www.vspublishers.com**

QUIZ BOOKS

ENGLISH IMPROVEMENT

OTHERS LANGUAGE ACTIVITIES BOOK QUOTES/SAYINGS

BIOGRAPHIES/CHILDREN SCIENCE LIBRARY

COMPUTER BOOKS

All books available at **www.vspublishers.com**

HINDI LITERATURE

TALES & STORIES

MUSIC (संगीत)

All Books Fully Coloured

MAGIC & FACT (जादू एवं तथ्य)

MYSTERIES (रहस्य)

ACADEMIC BOOKS

All books available at **www.vspublishers.com**

CAREER & BUSINESS MANAGEMENT

CONCISE DICTIONARIES

All books available at www.vspublishers.com

www.ingramcontent.com/pod-product-compliance
Lightning Source LLC
Chambersburg PA
CBHW070332230426
43663CB00011B/2285